Joy in Ministry

Joy in Ministry

*Messages from
Second Corinthians*

Michael Duduit

BAKER BOOK HOUSE
Grand Rapids, Michigan 49506

Contents

Acknowledgments

Appreciation is due to my wife, Laura, who has aided in so many ways in the preparation of this manuscript. She is friend, helper, co-minister, and a source of abundant joy in my life.

Special thanks are also due to the gracious congregation of West End Baptist Church in Birmingham, Alabama, to whom these messages were originally preached. Their support and encouragement have brought great joy as well.

Introduction

If modern-day Americans were to travel back in time to the first century A.D., they would probably be most at home in Corinth.

Corinth was a bustling center of commerce, a city of wealth and learning, a sophisticated, cosmopolitan city. Corinth was a melting pot, where Greeks, Romans, Jews, and many other peoples lived and worked together. We think of what it would have been like to live in Jerusalem or to walk the paths of Judea in Jesus' day, but the reality is that our experience would find much more in common with the people of Corinth.

Paul loved the Corinthian church dearly. He had been instrumental in its founding, and spent a year-and-a-half of his life living and working among them. He knew each of them by name. He knew what they were like: their strengths and weaknesses, their gifts and hurts. And still he loved them.

Yet few churches proved to be such a heartache to Paul. The First Epistle to the Corinthians is filled with correction and rebuke, aimed at moral failure and misplaced priorities. Though some good was accomplished through Paul's letter, we find Paul in this second letter sounding many of the same notes of concern and correction.

Despite the negative note of rebuke that often sounds in these pages, there is a positive note that is heard again and again—a theme that gives unity to the entire epistle—the joy of ministry. Above all Paul wants his beloved Corinthian believers to know the surpassing joy that comes from serving Christ.

Every man or woman who claims the name of Christ shares in a call to ministry. As Alan Redpath observes: "From the moment we receive Christ into our lives as Savior and Lord, life becomes a ministry. No longer is it an aimless existence to satisfy ourselves; it becomes a ministry for the blessing of other people."

And far from being a burden, this call to ministry is one of the great sources of joy in our Christian lives. In this Second Epistle to the Corinthians, Paul explores that tremendous theme in different ways, always returning to the same conclusion: there is no greater source of joy than serving Christ.

May the encouragement of our brother Paul touch our lives as well, and help us understand in a new and fresh way the joy of ministry.

1

Marks of a Servant
(2 Corinthians 1:3–11)

There are few things that appeal to us less than the idea of
being a servant.

Who wants to be a servant? Servants work hard taking
care of others' needs instead of their own. We might like to
have a servant, but we certainly don't want to *be* a servant!

If anything the past decade has reinforced those attitudes.
Oh, we're more than willing to go to a concert for African
hunger relief or make a pledge to help the homeless. We can
do those things and feel quite proud of ourselves. But we have
our limits—and they're rarely stretched.

Many of us might share the description George Eliot provided of a character in *Romala*: "He was to be depended on
to make any sacrifice that was not unpleasant."

Servanthood? Thanks, but no thanks.

So it comes as a bit of a shock to our systems to hear the
apostle Paul identify servanthood as one of the keys to joy in
ministry. Of course, that idea wasn't original with Paul. To
find the source of the idea, we need only to move back several
years earlier and observe Jesus instructing his disciples:

> ". . . whoever wants to become great among you must be your
> servant, and whoever wants to be first must be your slave—
> just as the Son of Man did not come to be served, but to serve,
> and to give his life as a ransom for many" (Matt. 20:26–28).

11

In an age when even the church throws the spotlight on celebrities and superstars, the idea of servanthood seems a bit out of place. Yet the message of Jesus, of Paul, of the gospel, is that ultimate joy and fulfillment emerge out of a life of service for Christ's sake.

So early in this letter to the troubled Corinthian church, Paul shares with them the marks of servanthood—those attributes that ought to characterize the life of one who follows Christ.

In an age when happiness is measured in clout rather than character, this is a message we need to hear. What are the marks of servanthood?

A Servant Undergoes Suffering for Others

These days we toss around the phrase "I'm suffering for Jesus," when we forego an extra doughnut or help in the nursery. Few Americans in the last quarter of the twentieth century have *any* idea what it means to suffer for their faith in Christ.

Paul knew. Open the Book of Acts almost anywhere and see Paul undergoing suffering, distress, and persecution as he carries out his missionary calling. In 2 Corinthians 1:8, 9 Paul describes a particular experience in Asia in which the suffering was so intense he felt death was imminent. While some have suggested this episode was some kind of illness or physical infirmity, Paul's comments and the context of the passage makes it more likely that he and his colleagues faced some external challenge related to their work.

Whatever the details, the apostle wants the Corinthian Christians to understand their own role in the story. As members of the body of Christ, the church, *they* benefited from his suffering. As he notes in verse 6, "If we are distressed, it is for your comfort and salvation. . . ."

Suffering for the sake of others is a mark of a servant. One familiar illustration of this principle is the process of childbirth. A mother goes through the pain of labor and delivery for the sake of giving birth to her child. Every one of us has benefited from our mothers' willingness to suffer on our behalf, in order that we might have life.

The ultimate example of this prinicple was provided when Jesus Christ hung upon a cross, suffering and dying, that we might have life. The Savior became a suffering servant for our sakes.

If we are to know the meaning of servanthood, here is our model: Christ gave himself for us. Will we give ourselves to him by giving *ourselves* for others? Are you and I willing to undergo difficulty, discomfort, suffering for the sake of others? For the sake of Christ?

During World War II, German pastor Martin Niemoeller took a courageous stand against Hitler—a stand that put him in a concentration camp. An American pastor visited with Martin's elderly parents, and they insisted, "When you go back to America, do not let anyone pity the father and mother of Martin Niemoeller. It is a terrible thing to have a son in a concentration camp. But there could be something more terrible for us: if God had needed a faithful martyr, and our Martin had been unwilling."

A Christian servant undergoes suffering for others. And because we suffer for others:

A Servant Provides Comfort to Others

What a wonderful promise is found in verses 3 and 4—and what a challenge!

Paul stresses first God's promise of comfort to his people. Though we experience distress, God is the "Father of compassion and the God of all comfort." He is the source of strength and encouragement that enables us to withstand the trials we face. He is the God of *all* comfort and he is able to comfort us in *all* our trials and difficulties. That covers every area of life; no matter what problem you face, no matter how intense your concern, God's comforting work is sufficient to meet your need.

Helmut Thielicke, in a sermon titled "The Mystery of Death," pointed to the miraculous power of God's comforting presence.

> Is it not strange that Christians on the sinking *Titanic* sang "Nearer, my God, to thee," and so lost their fear of drowning in the icy Atlantic? The point is that they did *not* sing, "Farther away are now the golden jewelry in my cabin, the precious documents in the ship's safe, farther away are my loved ones at home, farther than thousands of geographical miles—for now I must leave you forever." No, this is not what they sang or thought. It was not sad leave-taking and passing farther away; it was a coming nearer: "Nearer, my God, to thee."[1]

God provides abundant comfort to us. Yet Paul goes on to add an essential condition: God comforts us in order that we might comfort others. God's comforting has a purpose: to equip us for strengthening and encouraging others. The servant is comforted that he or she might become a comforter.

Here is an essential principle of the Christian life: God's provision for us is not for our benefit alone. What God gives us is not meant to be hoarded but *to be shared.* God loves us, and we are to love others. God comforts us—encourages us, strengthens us—and we are to comfort others.

Charles Colson was special counsel to President Richard M. Nixon, a position at the center of political power in the USA. His involvement in the Watergate cover-up led to his own arrest, conviction, and imprisonment—but the events of those days also led Chuck Colson to a personal faith in Jesus Christ.

Following his conversion, Colson was not miraculously freed from his own conviction; to the contrary, he was sent to Maxwell Federal Prison. Yet God was able to use that experience of imprisonment to open Colson's heart to the needs of prisoners, and to give him a special ministry to those men and women.

Colson himself puts it this way:

> *God often uses what we least expect for his divine purposes.*
> *That has certainly proved to be true for me. Out of the depths*

of my prison experience came the vision for Prison Fellow-ship's ministry, which now involves thousands of volunteers and brings the hope of Christ to prisoners throughout the U.S. and abroad. [2]

Chuck Colson's difficulty became a source of blessing to thousands of men and women behind bars who have been influenced for Christ. What a vivid example of Paul's assertion in verse 5:

For just as the sufferings of Christ flow over into our lives, so also through Christ our comfort overflows.

Each of us will undergo suffering in life; no life is immune from trial and difficulty. If we will allow him, Christ can take even that suffering and produce from it blessing in our lives and the lives of others. Even as God comforts us, our call is to reach out in love to bring comfort, strength, encouragement to others.

And because we allow God to use us in providing comfort to others:

A Servant Brings Hope to Others

G. K. Chesterton once observed: "There is one thing which gives radiance to everything. It is the idea of something around the corner."

We all need hope. We need a sense that there will be some meaning and purpose to it all, that something better is out there for us. In the absence of hope, it is no wonder that increasing numbers of people—including more and more teenagers—are giving up and taking their own lives. Without hope there *is* no life.

The servant of Christ is a carrier of hope. Because God's love has transformed our lives—bringing new hope, new meaning, new direction—we share that hope with others. What greater comfort can we give than hope?

Through his service to the Christians in Corinth, Paul had developed a steadfast hope on their behalf:

And our hope for you is firm, because we know that just as you share in our sufferings, so also you share in our comfort (v. 7).

According to Greek scholar A. T. Robertson, the word used here for *hope* carries with it the idea of waiting with expectation and patience.

Our hope is firm because of our confidence in God, the ultimate Source of all hope. Because of God's deliverance and the promise of his future care (v. 10), we have hope, confidence, assurance. The living, dynamic witness of Christ's servants produces that same powerful hope in the lives of others.

We have hope for today. Knowing we are in Christ, we can live confidently, trusting in his protection and guidance. No matter what trials life brings, the sense of his presence produces hope.

We also have hope for tomorrow. The future need not be a foreboding shadow that frightens us; to the contrary, Christ's followers enter the future with boldness. We do not fear the future because we know the future is securely in God's hands.

As servants of Christ, we not only *maintain* hope; we also *proclaim* hope. We announce the kingdom and invite others to enter its province, experiencing new hope in their own lives.

We are called to be servants of the Lord Jesus Christ; to be obedient to his call and faithful to his will. That call will carry us into a world of need, to undergo suffering as we bring comfort and hope to others. Yet always we must keep our focus on Jesus; he is the reason we minister.

A monk was complaining to Mother Teresa about some rules of his monastic order which he felt limited his ministry. "My vocation is to work for lepers," he said. "I want to spend myself for the lepers."

Mother Teresa corrected him: "Brother, your vocation is not to work for lepers; it is to belong to Jesus."

We serve others—undergoing suffering on their behalf, bringing comfort and hope—*because* we belong to Jesus. As we live out our servant's calling for him, the world will feel *his* touch in our hands and hear *his* voice in our words.

2

The Divine "Yes"
(2 Corinthians 1:15–22)

E. Stanley Jones spent a lifetime serving Christ as a missionary and evangelist. He spent more than half-a-century in India, and his evangelistic tours took him to many nations around the globe. He wrote twenty-eight books, including two best-sellers.

In December of 1971, when he was 87 years old, Jones had just finished his tenth evangelistic tour in Japan, speaking 154 times in 45 cities. Following the tour, he returned to the USA and was in Oklahoma City for a service he was to lead.

In the early morning hours of December 8, Jones experienced a paralyzing stroke. When his daughter reached his bedside in the hospital, the elderly evangelist signaled for her to draw near. In a feeble voice, he told her, "Daughter, I cannot die now. I have to live to complete another book—*The Divine Yes.*"[1]

In the fourteen remaining months of his life, E. Stanley Jones dictated the manuscript that would become that book: *The Divine Yes.* The title was taken from a sermon preached often by Jones, drawn from this text. More than a preached sermon, in those difficult months Jones literally *became* a sermon. His life became a resounding affirmation of the truth of the gospel—that in Christ, God has sounded an ultimate, final "yes."

The apostle Paul writes to a church that has questioned his character and his integrity. His original travel plans called for

18

two visits to Corinth, once on the way from Ephesus to Macedonia and a second visit on the return trip. Paul's travel plans changed however. Rather than going to Corinth twice, he only stopped one time during his journey to and from Macedonia.

There was a group in the church that was already antagonistic toward Paul, and this change of plans gave them an opportunity to unload on the apostle, spreading harsh criticism of him among other believers. He would say "yes" and "no" at the same time (v. 17), they claimed. He was fickle, unreliable, untrustworthy.

Have you ever been misunderstood and experienced unjust criticism as a result? You indicated you would do one thing, but someone thought you had said something altogether different, or perhaps circumstances required a change in plans? Then, when the originally planned action isn't carried out, you become a villain—the target of gossip and criticism about your unreliability or lack of commitment. Ever had that happen? Then you know a bit of how Paul feels as he writes to the church at Corinth.

As it turns out, Paul's change of plans was for *their* benefit (1:23—2:4). After the writing of First Corinthians, Paul paid a visit to Corinth that was apparently quite painful for him and for the church. To spare them another difficult visit so soon, Paul abandoned the planned second visit.[2]

In the midst of this discussion of his own integrity, Paul launches into a resounding affirmation of the One in whom we can place supreme confidence. Though men and women may disappoint us, may prove undependable or unreliable, we can place absolute trust in God, for he has confirmed his promises to us by providing the divine "Yes" in the Lord Jesus Christ.

Paul stresses that Christ is God's final answer to us. Whatever God has promised to his people finds its complete fulfillment in Christ. A survey of the Old Testament finds time after time prophesies are made about the coming Messiah that find their fulfillment in Christ.

Isaiah 7:14:

"Therefore the LORD himself will give you a sign: The virgin will be with child and will give birth to a son, and will call him Immanuel."

Isaiah 9:6, 7:

For to us a child is born,
to us a son is given,
and the government will be on his shoulders.
And he will be called
Wonderful Counselor, Mighty God,
Everlasting Father, Prince of Peace.
Of the increase of his government and peace
there will be no end.
He will reign on David's throne and over his kingdom,
establishing and upholding it
with justice and righteousness
from that time on and forever.
The zeal of the LORD Almighty will accomplish this.

Isaiah 53:3–5:

He was despised and rejected by men,
a man of sorrows, and familiar with suffering.
Like one from whom men hide their faces
he was despised, and we esteemed him not.
Surely he took up our infirmities
and carried our sorrows,
yet we considered him stricken by God,
smitten by him, and afflicted.
But he was pierced for our transgressions,
he was crushed for our iniquities;
the punishment that brought us peace
was upon him,
and by his wounds we are healed.

Micah 5:2:

"But you, Bethlehem Ephrathah,
though you are small among the clans of Judah,

out of you will come for me
one who will be ruler over Israel
whose origins are from of old,
from ancient times. "

Jesus Christ is God's "yes"—the ultimate affirmation of his love, his grace, his desire to draw us into relationship with himself.

Yet how do *we* experience that divine "yes" in our own lives? In these verses, Paul suggests four images that help us understand how God reaches out to us through Christ. In the first image Paul says:

We Are Guaranteed

Verse 21 can be translated a number of ways. The KJV says, "Now he which stablisheth us with you in Christ. . . ." The NEB translates it "And if you and we belong to Christ, guaranteed as his. . . ." C. K. Barrett puts it, "He who guarantees us."

The word which we translate "guarantee" or "establish" was a common term used in commercial and legal circles. Since Corinth was a bustling city of commerce, it would have been a frequently heard term—much as "buy" or "sell" might be used on Wall Street today.

The word was used to describe the closing of a sale, the confirmation of an agreement. It was a contractual word—a word that said each party would carry out the terms of an agreement. Have you ever signed a note to buy a car, or taken out a mortgage for a house? Then you have made just such a guarantee—at least the way the word was used in those days.

As happens throughout the New Testament, the writers take commonly used words and give them a deeper, more significant meaning. Paul takes a common business term and uses it to describe our personal relationship with God through Christ.

In Christ God has guaranteed our place within his family.
Jesus became a living affirmation of God's love and grace. On
the cross, he confirmed the new covenant with his own blood.

During the imperial reign of Napoleon Bonaparte, the
French army used a draft to fill its ranks. As was common in
other nations then—including the American Civil War—a
draftee was permitted to obtain a surrogate, a person who
would serve in his own place.

One young man who was drafted sought to avoid service,
and a friend volunteered to take the man's place. The substitute went into the army and was killed in battle. Some months
later, the same man was mistakenly drafted again. He went
to the army and said, "You can't draft me. I'm already dead."

"Are you insane?" asked the officer. "You are standing right
in front of me. You can't be dead!"

"Nevertheless," insisted the young man, "your records will
show that I died on the battlefield."

They did check, and sure enough, there was his name, with
another name written beside it. Since this seemed most un-
satisfactory, the case was taken before the Emperor Napoleon
himself. Examining the facts of the case, the emperor announced that through a substitute the young man had already fought and died for France. Napoleon said, "No man can
die more than once, therefore the law has no claim on him."

On the cross, Jesus Christ gave his life on our behalf. He
guaranteed our relationship as children of God. There is nothing more for us to do to guarantee that relationship, for Christ
has done it all in his own death and resurrection.

There's a second image Paul provides in this same
verse (21):

He Anoints Us

The name *Christ* is literally the Greek term for "anointed
one." Acts 10:38 tells us, ". . . God anointed Jesus of Nazareth
with the Holy Spirit and with power. . . ." Anointing involves
recognizing and setting aside for a divine purpose.

What does it mean, then, when Paul tells us as believers that God has anointed us?

First, *it means we have been called for service.* God has placed his hand on us to set us aside for his purposes. The anointing of Messiah was an anointing to a function, a purpose; likewise, we are anointed to service on Christ's behalf. We share, in a small way, in Christ's anointing because we are in him. We are also "anointed ones."

Following World War II, the residents of Strasbourg, France, began searching through the rubble of what had once been their church. Amidst the rubble of that bombed-out structure they found a statue of Christ which was intact except for the two outstretched hands, which had been destroyed.

There was much discussion among the church members about the possibility of having the statue repaired or replaced, to restore the missing hands. Eventually, they decided to leave the statue as it was, as a reminder that Christ uses *our* hands to reach out to a hurting world.

Because we share in his anointing, we have been called to serve Christ. Second, *through our anointing we have been equipped for service.*

C. K. Barrett, a New Testament scholar, points out that the anointing of Messiah implies not only his election for service but also "His equipment for carrying out the work to which He is called."[3] We are anointed for service, and that very anointing involves God equipping us for service.

God does not call us and then abandon us. Whatever the task God has called you to do, he will also give you the power and gifts required to perform the work—even though you may not realize they are even there.

In the thick fog, a ship lost its way near the harbor and became lodged on a reef during low tide. The tug boats steamed to the rescue, but try as they might they couldn't budge the great ship from its captivity on that reef. The captain waved the tugs away, and began to wait. Hours later, as if held by an unseen power, the ship began to inch higher as the tide moved in. What a dozen tug boats couldn't accomplish was done by the power of the tide as it lifted the ship.

So it is with the power of God in our lives. As he anoints us, he also provides that which we need to serve effectively. What we could never do in our own power is done in *his* power. That is one of the secrets to our joy in ministry.

He Seals Us

In verse 22, Paul says God "set his seal of ownership on us. . . ." Like the first image we saw—that of the guarantee— the image of the seal is also drawn from the commercial and legal world of Paul's day.

A seal had two purposes on a document. First it was a sign of ownership. By placing my seal on a document, I am acknowledging my ownership of the property or transaction. When you see my seal on the contract, you have my guarantee as to the authenticity of the document; it is no forgery.

A seal was also used to protect documents from tampering. By placing my seal on the outside of a document, others are unable to alter it while in transit. The broken seal would be evidence of such tampering.

When Paul says God has sealed us with his Holy Spirit, it indicates that God has placed his mark of ownership upon us. God has clearly identified us as his own property. We belong to him, and the seal of the Spirit in our lives is evidence of that ownership.

One of the popular methods of putting your individual stamp on your car these days is through a personalized license tag. Most states will allow you to pay an extra fee and write your own six- or seven-letter message for your car tag. Some people use it to identify their occupations—like DOCTOR or SALES-1—while others use it to display a hobby or even their own names. It's a way of saying, "This car is *mine.*"

When you commit your life to Christ as Lord and Savior, God places his Spirit in your life as a way of saying, "This man, this woman, belongs to me."

Not only is the seal of the Spirit a sign of God's ownership, it is also a protection. Like protecting a document from those who would tamper with it, the Holy Spirit becomes a protective seal to keep you secure and safe within God's care. That is what Paul is referring to in Ephesians 4:30, when he says, "And do not grieve that Holy Spirit of God, with whom you were sealed for the day of redemption."

The presence of God's Spirit in our lives is an evidence of God's ownership and of his protection. Finally, Paul says, the presence of the Spirit means:

He Has Given a Pledge to Us

The word found in the latter part of verse 22 is normally translated "earnest" or "deposit." As A. T. Robertson points out, the word was commonly used in Paul's day "as earnest money in a purchase for a cow or for a wife (a dowry)."[4]

It referred to a down payment—an initial payment made as evidence of good faith, to show that the purchaser would complete the transaction. Even today, when purchasing a new home, the real estate agent will explain the need to provide five hundred or one thousand dollars in "earnest money" along with the sales contract as evidence of the integrity of your offer. By providing such a deposit, you show a willingness to carry through on your commitment.

God's gift of the Holy Spirit is one way of assuring us of his love and provision for us, not only in the present age but also in the age to come. As we live now in the power of the Holy Spirit, we experience a mere taste of what that greater life will be in the age to come. The Holy Spirit is a deposit, a pledge of blessings yet to come.

A young couple begins the task of house hunting. They look through house after house until—finally—they walk into one that puts a sparkle in their eyes. "This is the *one*," they exclaim. As they make an offer to buy the house, they enclose a deposit, *earnest money* representing their good faith interest in buying the house.

So much is wrapped up in that deposit: their dreams of a new home, commitment to complete the purchase, eager expectations of life in that home for many years to come. It is a significant event in their lives.

God has made an even greater commitment to us; he has said "yes" to you and me. Through Christ's death and resurrection, he has guaranteed us as his own, and he has anointed us for service to him. Through the gift of the Holy Spirit in our lives, he has sealed us and given us a taste of the age to come. Over and over, God has said "yes" to us. In every need, every hurt, every dream of life, God's response is a powerful *yes* through Jesus Christ.

E. Stanley Jones—in that same book, *The Divine Yes*—told of a Christian woman who was an invalid. She had a ministry of writing letters to prisoners in Japanese jails. She wrote one letter to a well-known prisoner being tried for murder. That letter was used by God to touch the man deeply, and through her influence he was led to Christ.

The prisoner became a dynamic servant for Christ, leading many other prisoners to the Lord. When the day of his execution came, this condemned man had communion with a pastor at the base of the scaffold. Then he told the officials gathered around: "You are not executing the man who did the deed, for he is already dead. He is risen in this new man who stands before you and is willing to take the penalty for the dead man and be buried with Christ. But I am not the same man."

The prison officials were visibly shaken, but not the prisoner. As the trap door was released to drop the man to his death, onlookers heard him singing "Nearer My God to Thee."[5]

The power of Christ takes a human "no" and transforms it into a divine "yes." It does not matter how many "nos" the world is throwing in your path; today you can hear and respond to the divine "yes" that will transform your life.

3

The Fragrance of Christ
(2 Corinthians 2:14–17)

The Roman Empire was built at the point of a sword.

Led by her generals, Rome's armies conquered Europe, the Middle East, and the north of Africa. One of the most vivid experiences a citizen of Rome would ever observe was the triumphal procession of a victorious general and his army.

The triumphal march was only permitted to the general whose campaign had been particularly successful. He must have added territory to the Empire, pacified the region, and returned to Rome with his troops. He must have had at least one battle in which five thousand of the enemy had been killed.

William Barclay describes the triumphal procession which made its way through the streets of Rome:

> First there came the state officials and the senate. Then there came the trumpeters. Then there were carried the spoils taken from the conquered land. . . . Then there came pictures of the conquered land and models of conquered citadels and ships. There followed the white bull for the sacrifice which would be made.
>
> Then there walked the wretched captives, the enemy princes, leaders and generals in chains, shortly to be flung in prison and in all probability almost immediately to be executed. Then there came the lictors bearing their rods, followed by the musicians with their lyres. Then there came the priests swinging their censers with the sweet-smelling incense burning in them.
>
> And then there came the general himself. He stood in a char-

iot drawn by four horses. . . . After him there rode his family,
and finally there came the army wearing all their decorations
and shouting *Io triumphe!* their cry of triumph.[1]

What a sight that must have been! A New York ticker-tape
parade or a Fourth of July fireworks show wouldn't hold a
candle to such a procession for the amazing spectacle and
majesty of the event.

The apostle Paul, who has been sharing with the Corinthian church the burdens and difficulties of his ministry, suddenly stops and begins an entirely new line of thought. He
proclaims the glorious joy of sharing in Christ's ministry, using the triumphal procession of a Roman general as an illustration of Christ's victory and the joy *we* experience in ministry
as his followers.

As ministers of Christ—and every disciple is called to service and ministry in his name—we share in the triumph of
Christ. Like a Roman Legion marching behind its general, we
as Christ's followers march with him in the victorious procession that leads from Calvary to the empty tomb, and ultimately to his glorious return at the end of the age.

Out of that event of the triumphal procession, Paul draws
a particular element to further illustrate our role as servants
of the kingdom. During the triumphal procession, the temples of Rome were filled with the fragrance of burning incense,
and in the processional itself bearers carried burning incense
ahead of the conquering general.[2]

Paul says that *we* are bearers of the fragrance of Christ;
even more, we have become the very fragrance of Christ. As
the NEB translates it, "We are indeed the incense offered by
Christ to God."

What does Paul mean when he calls us "the fragrance of
Christ"? What characteristics are we to have? First, Paul says:

We Are to Be a Pleasing Fragrance

In verse 14, the word *fragrance* is translated "sweet odour"
(TWENTIETH CENTURY NEW TESTAMENT); "sweet savour" (C. K.
Barrett); or "lovely perfume" (PHILLIPS).

Paul almost certainly had in mind here not only the incense of the Roman Triumph but also the idea of sacrifice to God. Again and again in the Old Testament, sacrifices offered to God are described as a "fragrance pleasing to God." In Genesis 8, Noah sacrificed a burnt offering to God, and verse 21 says, "The LORD smelled the pleasing aroma." When God gave Moses instructions for consecrating priests, Exodus 29:18 directed Aaron to burn a ram on the altar, saying "It is a burnt offering to the LORD, a pleasing aroma. . . ." Leviticus 1:9 offers instructions for making a burnt offering to God: "an aroma pleasing to the LORD."

This idea of a sacrifice as a fragrant offering to God enters the New Testament in Ephesians 5:2, where Paul challenges us to "live a life of love, just as Christ loved us and gave himself up for us as a fragrant offering and sacrifice to God."

What does it mean, then, *to be a pleasing fragrance?* It means to offer oneself as a sacrifice to God—to yield ourselves on the altar of commitment and service. As Paul says in Romans 12:1, we are to offer ourselves as "living sacrifices, holy and pleasing to God. . . ."

We pride ourselves on our "sacrificial" offerings to God. If we tithe 10 percent of our income to God's work, we consider ourselves unusually sacrificial—and an offering above the tithe nearly qualifies us for sainthood! Likewise we so often think of "sacrifice" in terms of accepting some place of service in the church or giving our time to some mission project or activity.

The truth is, God never asks us to put our time, talents, or treasure on the altar as sacrifices. He asks us to crawl onto that altar ourselves; *we* must become the sacrifice. God demands all that we are be offered to him—that alone is the sacrifice that is pleasing to him. When we give God our lives, the other things take care of themselves.

John Hancock was president of the Continental Congress during the American Revolution, as well as one of the signers of the Declaration of Independence. Boston was under British control, and General George Washington consulted congress about the advisability of bombarding the city. One member made a motion that the congress seek the opinion of Mr. Hancock, since all of his property was located in Boston. A heavy bombardment might leave him financially ruined.

Hancock responded: "It is true, sir, nearly all of the property I have in the world is in houses and other real estate in the town of Boston; but if the liberties of our country require their being burnt to ashes—issue the order for that purpose immediately!"

God is seeking men and women who will say: "Whatever the cost, whatever the demands, my life belongs to Christ." That is the sacrifice that is a pleasing fragrance in the presence of God.

We Are to Be a Penetrating Fragrance

As the triumphal procession made its way through the streets of Rome, the fragrance of burning incense was felt all along the way. Throughout the crowds, the sweet odor was making its impact.

As those who carry the fragrance of Christ, we are to carry it everywhere. Verse 14 notes that God, "through us spreads everywhere the fragrance of the knowledge of him." The Twentieth Century New Testament says God "uses us to spread the sweet odour of the knowledge of him in every place."

As soldiers of Rome extended the empire throughout their world, soldiers of Christ carry the good news of God's love and grace. We have the privilege of being the instruments through whom the gospel is shared with a world in need.

How do we share that good news? One way is *visually*: we allow our lives to be a living witness to the power of Christ.

Palmer Ofuoku is a pastor in Nigeria. Although his family was not Christian, they sent Palmer to a mission school to receive an education. For a number of years he attended the school, encountering a variety of missionaries who assumed a dominant attitude toward the Nigerians. The young man was not attracted by that kind of Christianity.

Then a new missionary arrived who gave himself in loving concern for the Nigerian students. He built caring relationships with students, and eventually led many of them to Christ—including Palmer.

Years later, Palmer testified to the influence of that missionary, saying: "He built a bridge of friendship to me, and Jesus walked across."[3] As we offer ourselves as living sacrifices to Christ, we will also build bridges that will allow Jesus to walk across.

Yet our witness is not only visual; it must also be *verbal*. We *show* Christ's love in action, then *share* it.

John Bunyan, who wrote *Pilgrim's Progress*, was led to Christ by hearing three women talk joyfully of their relationship with Christ. William Carey, the father of modern missions, came to know Christ through the witness of a fellow apprentice shoe cobbler. Charles H. Spurgeon came to know Christ through the message of an unknown, uneducated lay preacher.

We do not know how God will use our witness; he simply asks us to be faithful in sharing the good news we have already received. Thus the fragrance of Christ is spread throughout a lost and dying world.

We are called to be a pleasing fragrance and a penetrating fragrance for Christ. Further:

We Are to Be a Powerful Fragrance

As the Roman armies marched in a triumphal procession, the aroma of burning incense would have a different effect on different persons. To the soldiers who had fought victoriously and the crowd that welcomed the army home, it was a sweet smell of triumph. But to the captives who marched in chains—and who faced either slavery or death at the end of the procession—it was a bitter aroma, for it was the smell of defeat and death.

As we carry the fragrance of Christ everywhere, we realize that some receive it positively while others refuse it. As verse 16 says, "To the one we are the smell of death; to the other, the fragrance of life. . . ."

The same message can be both healing or poisonous, depending on the attitude of the hearer. The news of the end of a battle will bring joy to one side in the conflict and sadness to the other. Paul would have been familiar with the way in which the rabbis described the Torah (the Law) in this way— it was an elixir of life to Israel but poison to the other nations that rejected it.

The New Testament describes Christ in much the same terms. He is the cornerstone of faith for those who believe, but a stumbling-stone for those who reject him. The message we carry as the fragrance of Christ is a powerful one, for it is a message of life or death.

No wonder Paul wonders, "Who is equal to such a task?" (v. 16). Clearly none of us is worthy in and of ourselves to carry such a significant message. We are all inadequate for the task. That is why Paul says:

We Are to Be a Pure Fragrance

Because eternal destinies are in the balance, God calls us to be pure messengers of his Word, serving in a spirit of sincerity and humility. Paul knew that he was incapable of being a worthy messenger of Christ in his own power; he could only do so "in Christ"—in the power and strength of the Lord Jesus Christ working in and through him.

There were some who "peddled the word of God for profit" (*see* v. 17). The allusion was to the unscrupulous wine merchants in Paul's day who would pour water into the wine, adulterating the product for the sake of an extra profit. Paul said, in effect, there were those within the church who "watered down" the gospel—ignoring its demands, simply telling the people what they wanted to hear, in order that they might be more generous in their offerings.

Some things never change, do they? Those same preachers of a "watered-down" gospel continue to tickle our ears with pretty, pious phrases while ignoring the heart of the gospel. They tell us we can have salvation without service, Christ without commitment, church without challenge. If we are to be the fragrance of Christ, we are called to handle the Word of God purely, honestly; to allow the Word to shape us and change us to be more like Jesus.

If you visit Rome today, you can see many of the places where those victorious generals marched. You can see where the temples stood and the incense burned. Unfortunately today most of those great monuments lie in ruins—columns broken and spread along the ground, marble peeled away, shattered stones scattered and gone. Those great generals went to their tombs centuries ago, their armies gone, their triumphs long since erased.

Yet the triumphant procession of Christ and his church continues day after day, century after century. You and I are invited to be part of this joyful procession—joining with Christ, becoming his fragrance, his messengers, to a world in need. Will you come and march with him?

4

A Letter of Christ
(2 Corinthians 3:1–3)

If you've ever applied for a job, you've probably been asked to supply a letter of recommendation. Your prospective employer wants a letter from someone who knows you well, one which will shed some light on your attitude, skills, and work habits.

Of course employers these days have to be careful in evaluating such letters. Since writers of negative recommendations have been sued on more than one occasion, it's getting increasingly difficult to get an honest evaluation from former employers.

An article in one business magazine even offered a series of phrases which, though appearing to sound positive, actually carry negative hidden meanings. For example, you might write of a lousy employee: "I just can't say enough good things about this person." The writer of such a letter may be saying he can't say enough good things because there aren't any good things to be said!

In Paul's day, travelers commonly carried with them letters of commendation. For example, a merchant might be traveling from Rome to Corinth. He would find a friend who had associates in Corinth and ask this person to write a letter of commendation, testifying to his identity and character. Upon his arrival in Corinth, the merchant would seek out his contact and present the letter as a means of introduction to the community.

The same thing happened in the New Testament. At the beginning of Romans 16, Paul writes a letter of commendation for Phoebe, asking that she be received warmly and helped in her work. In the eighth chapter of this very letter of Second Corinthians, Paul includes a commendation of Titus and his companions, who would be carrying the letter to Corinth.

These letters were very important in the early church because of the abundance of charlatans who sought to live off the generosity of the churches. Even in the fifth century, the Council of Chalcedon declared that "strange and unknown clerics were under no circumstances whatever to minister in another city without epistles commendatory from their own bishop."[1]

In chapter 2, Paul referred to those who were "peddling the gospel" for their own profit. Some of these phony missionaries carried letters from other churches where they had visited, and they had asked the Corinthian church to provide such reference letters for them. Apparently they had criticized Paul as someone who carried no such letters on his behalf.

Paul noted that Corinth was the last place on earth where he should need letters of commendation. After all, most of them had become believers through his ministry among them. He was their spiritual father, and they were his children in the Lord. Paul carried the Corinthian Christians in his heart. Literally, *they* were his letter of commendation.

What a tremendous thought this is for all who minister in Jesus' name! When God uses you to lead someone to faith in Christ, that new believer becomes a letter of commendation— a visible expression of God's work through you.

At verse 3, however, Paul takes the idea of letter and develops a new thought altogether. As Christians, Paul says, *we* are Christ's letters of commendation. We have become living letters which express the mind of Christ. Notice three key ideas present in the verse:

We Are Written by Christ

The Corinthian church was a letter written by Christ. Though Paul's influence was evident, Christ alone was the author of their salvation. Each believer is a letter of Christ.

That is also true of us. You and I—if we have given our lives to Christ—are living letters, giving testimony wherever we go to the One who has redeemed us and placed his imprint upon our lives.

Have you ever written a love letter? Some of us began writing love letters in grade school—passing those notes across the classroom from desk to desk. (We were mortified if someone else intercepted the message and read it!) Some of us perhaps still write an occasional love letter.

Certainly we can enjoy the beauty of love letters written in years gone by. There is always great interest in such letters written by Lincoln or Washington or other well-known figures. Perhaps we are fascinated with such letters because they reveal something very real about the life and thought of the writer.

As letters written by Christ, the world looks at us and reads about Jesus. Our lives serve as the only gospel most people will ever read.

A TV repairman kept putting off repairing his own television antenna after a storm tore off one of its arms. When a new family moved in next door, the man decided to install his own antenna. He knew the neighbor was a TV repairman so he modeled his own installation after the expert's. He drilled the hole in the same location and turned the antenna in the same direction. Carefully studying his neighbor's roof, he finally reached up and tore the arm off his brand-new antenna![2]

Believe it not, you and I are the experts on Christianity in this world—at least according to those who watch us every day. We are letters written by Christ—expressions of his love, his grace, his concern. How tragic if they receive a faulty impression of the living Lord because of the message we offer with *our* lives.

Will you let the authentic Christ be seen in *your* life? Will you allow his love to be written in *your* actions, *your* words, *your* attitudes, so that in you people might see the good news of Christ?

We are letters written by Christ. Further:

We Are Letters Written
with the Holy Spirit

Do you remember playing with disappearing ink when you were young? What fun we would have writing notes that would then disappear from the page completely! Recently news reports indicate a modern—and costly—version of the old disappearing-ink trick. The culprits treated checks with some type of chemical prior to cashing them; then within hours, the checks would begin to disintegrate before the bank would have charged them against the account. Some of us know what it's like to have our bank account disappear, but banks don't take kindly to having the tables turned!

The point is, even so-called permanent ink isn't really permanent. It can burn, fade, perish. The letter Christ writes in our lives is not written with perishable ink but with the Holy Spirit. The letter Christ writes in our lives is not temporal but permanent, eternal, because it is written with the Holy Spirit.

When you receive Christ as Savior and Lord, it is the Holy Spirit who draws you to Christ and works in you to accomplish the work of redemption. That is why in Romans 5:5, Paul says, ". . . God has poured out his love into our hearts by the Holy Spirit, whom he has given us." I like Moffatt's translation also: "since God's love floods our hearts through the Holy Spirit."

It is the Spirit who assists us in prayer (Rom. 8:26), provides us with the elements needed for victorious Christian living (Gal. 5:22, 23), and seals us as a guarantee of eternal life (Eph. 1:14). As the Spirit works in us to shape us more and more in the image of Christ, we become better vehicles for transmitting the gospel to a lost world. The letter Christ writes in us becomes clearer.

The writing of the Spirit in our lives does not fade away but abides eternally. The transforming work of the Spirit in our lives changes us forever. That is why Paul can say of this letter of Christ:

We Are Letters Written from Within

In Exodus 31:18, we read that God gave the law to Moses inscribed on two tablets of stone. At Sinai God gave an external set of laws which mankind found itself utterly incapable of fully obeying. Men and women were never able to fulfill the obligations of the old covenant.

In chapter 31 of Jeremiah, the prophet points to a time when God would establish a new covenant with his people. In the covenant, the Lord declares, ". . . I will put my law in their minds and write it on their hearts . . ." (v. 33). Under this new covenant, the law would no longer be simply an external set of regulations but would become an inward principle. Through the indwelling Spirit, the law of Christ would become a vital, dynamic force within us.

That is the letter Christ has written on our hearts. God has written his truth on our hearts, and it is to be reflected in the things we do and say. The gospel is not simply a collection of printed pages; *it is the power of God working in your life and mine.*

The musical performer Arthur Rubenstein continued to delight and inspire audiences into his 80s. Asked one time how he continued to keep his performances fresh and alive, he responded, "Every day I am a new man, and every occasion is a new moment for me. When I play, it is no longer I, but a secret power that takes over."

That is also the key to the abundant Christian life: there is a power that wells up from inside of us and makes available to us the resources of heaven. That power is within us because Christ has placed it in our hearts through the Holy Spirit. We are his living letters. The change in our lives is evidence to the world that we serve a risen Lord.

From time to time we hear news reports of one of the famous auction houses selling an original letter by a famous person. Depending on the kind of letter it is, an original, handwritten letter—by a Lincoln or a Jefferson or a Washington—can bring a sales price in the tens of thousands of dollars.

Yet the most precious letter in all the world is the letter Christ has written in your heart through the Holy Spirit. Will you allow the world to read that letter in your life—to see Christ in you?

5

When the Veil Is Lifted
(2 Corinthians 3:12–18)

Math was always my worst subject. I loved history—learning about great people and important events and how we came to be where we are today. I enjoyed geography—countries and oceans and maps, even learning state capitals. I even liked English—learning how to write and communicate more effectively; then reading stories by those who had learned those lessons well.

But math was something else entirely. Simple arithmetic wasn't so bad; I didn't mind addition and subtraction, since I could see how I'd use it in buying and selling. I memorized my multiplication tables: 1 times 1; 2 times 2; 12 times 12; and so on.

It was when we got to percentages that I realized math might give me problems. Then came algebra and geometry, and from that point on I was in trouble. Sometimes I would sit and stare at the page for the longest time, wondering if anything would ever jump off that page and into my brain!

I understand that in mathematics—as perhaps in other fields—there's something called the "eureka experience." The word comes from the exclamation that gold miners would shout when they struck gold. Shaking their pan over a stream, they'd spot nuggets of gold among the silt and they'd shout, "Eureka! I've found it!"

Something of that process takes place in learning math. You may study and analyze a problem for hours, and it may still seem like Greek. Then all at once, it is as if a giant curtain is raised in your mind to reveal the principle by which the problem can be solved. Suddenly, your mind shouts, *Eureka! I've found it!* You still have to work through the problem, but now you understand *how* to solve it. You've had a "eureka experience."

In the verses preceding our text, Paul has begun contrasting the old covenant—the one God gave through Moses and the law—and the new covenant, initiated through Christ. Although there was glory in the old covenant, the verses in our text explain the reasons for that greater glory of the new covenant.

Chapter 34 of Exodus, which tells of Moses receiving the covenant law from God, indicates that after Moses left the presence of God and came down from Sinai, his face was radiant from the continuing reflection of God's glory. After speaking to the people, Moses placed a veil over his face (Exod. 34:33).

Paul explains here (v. 13) that Moses used a veil to cover his face so that the Israelites would not see the radiance as it faded away. Perhaps Moses felt they would lose faith in him if they watched the radiance slowly fade from his face; perhaps, instead, he felt the people's disobedience made them unworthy to see the Lord's reflected glory, except as he was actually speaking God's words to the people.

The important point in Paul's view was that the radiance *did* fade. Though Moses' face reflected the glory of God immediately after a personal encounter, the reflection inevitably faded from his face. And that, Paul says, is symbolic of the old covenant itself—it was always meant to be temporary, a fading glory that would be overshadowed by the new covenant in the Lord Jesus Christ. The old covenant was not bad; it was simply incomplete. Completion came in the new covenant, which we find through Christ.

In the new covenant, Paul says, the veil is lifted to reveal the glorious presence of God—a presence and radiance that will never fade. And the veil is lifted only by Christ (v. 14).

What happens when the veil is lifted?

When the Veil Is Lifted,
There Is Understanding

In mathematics, the "eureka experience" is when the veil is lifted and we understand the principle we are studying. When we surrender our lives to the Lord Jesus Christ, we undergo a spiritual "eureka experience," as the veil is lifted and new understanding enters our lives.

As we enter into a relationship with Christ, things that were obscure before suddenly become clear. The man or woman without Christ must look on at what we do here in the church and observe: "How absurd! Why would they give up a Sunday morning of sleep to get up early, get dressed up, and spend it in singing hymns and listening to some loud-mouthed preacher? Why would they give away 10 percent—or even more—of their income? Why would they give their time and energy for so many causes?"

Have you ever thought about how foolish it must seem to someone who doesn't know Christ? No wonder we don't win people to church; only when a person has come to know Christ does church make much sense. The veil must be lifted before understanding comes.

Only in Christ do the truths of God's Word really begin to make an impact in our lives. It is only in relationship to Jesus that the meaning of Scripture becomes clear.

That's what Paul is saying in verses 14 and 15.

Because of their disobedience in Moses' day, the children of Israel allowed a veil to obscure even the old covenant. Because of unrepentant hearts, the people had uncomprehending minds. Their sin destroyed their spiritual vision.

The great tragedy, Paul says in verse 15, is that even into his own day, the same veil obscured God's Word from this people. As C. K. Barrett notes, "The Torah (or law) contained the truth, but it could not penetrate through the veil to the hearers' heart."[1]

Not only did a veil block Israel from understanding the old

covenant—the double tragedy is that they were also unable—
or unwilling—to gaze on the greater glory of the new covenant. As Jesus himself said, "If you believed Moses you would
believe me, for he wrote about me. But since you do not believe
what he wrote, how are you going to believe what I say?" (John
5:46, 47).

Only as we open our hearts to Jesus Christ will our minds
be opened to greater understanding of God's truth.

If you have seen the play or the movie *The Miracle Worker*,
you know that it is the story of teacher Anne Sullivan and her
pupil, Helen Keller. Helen was both blind and deaf; in their
sympathy for Helen's plight, her family was unwilling to ex-
tend any real discipline to her. Unseeing, unhearing, and un-
controlled, Helen was like a frantic, frightened animal.

One day Anne Sullivan, a new teacher, arrived. Realizing
that nothing could be accomplished while the family was
around forbidding discipline, Miss Sullivan took Helen away
for her lessons. She knew that the only way to get through to
Helen was to open up some line of communication, but the
child's dual disability made sign language more complicated.

Day after day, Anne Sullivan tried to help Helen understand
the relationship between the objects she touched and the words
the teacher signed in Helen's palm. Yet it was as if a veil hid
the meaning from Helen's mind.

Then it happened. Miss Sullivan placed Helen's hands under
flowing water from the pump, and signed the word *water* into
Helen's palm. It was as if a veil was lifted when Helen slowly
repeated the sign for *water* back into Anne Sullivan's palm.
The barrier was broken down and a new world opened up to
Helen Keller.

When we allow Christ to come into our hearts and lives,
the veil is lifted and a new understanding of God's love and
God's truth becomes part of us. Suddenly new truths begin
to spring forth from God's Word; new insights seem so obvious
and clear.

Paul notes yet another result:

When the Veil Is Lifted,
There Is Freedom

". . . where the Spirit of the Lord is, there is freedom" (v. 17).

As we turn to Christ in repentance and faith, the veil is lifted to reveal a new relationship with God—a relationship based not on law but on love. We find new freedom in Christ.

The old covenant was dominated by obedience to a code of laws. Under the old covenant, men and women were bound to external commands, carved in stone or written on paper.

By contrast the new covenant in Christ is a relationship based in love and freedom. Obedience is present, but as a loving response to God's grace rather than a grudging adherence to God's commands. In Christ we are freed from law, from sin, from death—freed to love and serve as children and heirs.

What brings about the change? Whereas the old covenant was written in stone, the new covenant is written in our hearts. The Spirit of God comes to dwell in our hearts, producing a desire to follow Christ in faithful obedience. It is no longer law that binds us but love.

Even within the church we sometimes surrender our freedom on behalf of legalism. All too often, churches and individual Christians become captive to lists of rules, to tradition, to a negative spirit. We succumb to the dry rot of religious practice and self-righteous attitudes. What a tragedy that, like Esau, we would sell our birthright for something worth so little.

The landscape of our era is littered with the remains of liberation movements. *Liberation* is the password of the twentieth century. We've seen women's liberation, the Palestine Liberation Organization, the liberation theologians, and much more. Some uses of the term *liberation* have been good and positive; others cynical and evil.

Yet the most important liberation movement in history began, not in our century, but two thousand years ago—in the death and resurrection of Jesus Christ. For it is only in relationship to Christ that the veil is lifted; only in Christ are we freed from the bondage of sin and death, of legalism and religiosity; freed to live abundantly in the power of the Spirit. Because Christ has lifted the veil to offer us understanding and freedom, there is yet another result:

When the Veil Is Lifted, There Is Christ-likeness

Verse 18 is one place where a quick reading of the KJV might lead us astray. The phrase "beholding as in a glass the glory of the Lord" would suggest we are looking through a glass to see the Lord. But the original has quite a different meaning. Rather than translating it "beholding as in a glass," we are more accurate in saying we are to "reflect" the glory of the Lord. PHILLIPS put it like this: "All of us who are Christians have no veils on our faces, but reflect like mirrors the glory of the Lord."

A mirror reflects only what is before it. The moon has no light of its own, but brightens the night sky by reflecting the sun's light. So it is that you and I—when the veil has been lifted—are able to reflect the glory of the Lord in our own lives.

Of his generation, only Moses was permitted to enter directly into the presence of God. In Christ each of us has been given that privilege. And like Moses coming from the presence of God on Sinai, when we have been with Jesus there is a reflection of his glory present in our lives. Alan Redpath observes:

> The man who gazes upon and contemplates day by day the face of the Lord Jesus Christ, and who has caught the glow of the reality that the Lord is not a theory but an indwelling power and force in his life, is a mirror reflecting the glory of the Lord. Wherever he goes, people begin to ask questions as to why he triumphs when others fail . . . how it is, when facing buffeting of one kind or another, he reacts with such patience; how it is, when the general level of conversation is so impure he is never

dragged down, and how he stands above it, not in a sense of
rebuke to others but in a sense of testimony to the fact that,
because he belongs to God, he cannot descend to another level.
He has caught the glow and is reflecting it. . . .[2]

Something else happens when we spend time with Jesus:
we become more like him. Paul says we "are being transformed into his likeness with ever-increasing glory . . ." (v. 18).

As we look on his glory, as we spend time in the Lord's
presence, our lives are shaped and molded by the Holy Spirit
into the image of Christ. We begin to love people as he loved
them; we begin to treat others the way he treated them; we
begin to obey the Father the way he obeyed the Father. Day by
day, we become more and more like Jesus.

Adoniram and Ann Judson were missionaries in Burma.
One day Ann was reading some newspaper clippings about
their work; thinking it might amuse him, she pointed out to
Judson that one of the clippings compared him to one of the
apostles.

Rather than amusement, the thought bothered Judson
greatly. Finally he explained to his wife, "I do not want to be
like them. I do not want to be like Paul, nor Apollos, nor
Cephas, nor any mere man. I want to be like Christ."

Because the veil has been lifted—because we have been
permitted into the very presence of God through Christ—it is
our privilege and our challenge to be more like Jesus.

When the people of Jerusalem encountered the apostles in
those early days after Pentecost, they observed, "Surely these
men have been with Jesus" (Acts 4:13). May the same be said
of us.

6

We Have This Treasure
(2 Corinthians 4:1–7)

You may have read in the newspaper the story of a rock collector in Chattanooga, Tennessee. He was at a flea market, browsing through the items on display, when he came across a big blue rock for sale as a paperweight. He thought it was attractive, so he bought it for a couple of dollars.

Later he decided to have the rock checked out to determine what kind of mineral it was. To his astonishment, the flea-market rock was, in fact, a massive sapphire worth tens of thousands of dollars. What had been valueless the day before was now understood to be of tremendous value.

In this passage Paul wants the Christians at Corinth to understand the incredible treasure that had been placed in their hands. What was this treasure? It was their status as ministers of the Lord Jesus Christ.

If you have given your life to Jesus Christ as Lord and Savior, you also have this treasure, this ministry, in your life. What does it mean for us to be ministers of Christ?

We Have a Divine Call

The same God who saved you—who forgave your sin, redeemed you, and now indwells you—calls you to be his minister.

It is not an optional call. When you are buying a new car, you pick and choose among any number of options—yes, I'll

47

take air conditioning; no, I'll pass on the rear-window defogger; sure, might as well add the reclining bucket seats.

Unfortunately, some Christians act as if the call to ministry is optional, like so many features in a car. When God reached out to redeem us, he saved us to serve. As Paul says, we *have* this ministry. It is ours because God has called us.

It is not a deserved call. There is nothing in us that makes us worthy of the treasure of serving Christ. You and I do not deserve to be ministers, but God has bestowed the privilege of service on each one who claims Christ as Lord. That's why Paul says in verse 1: "since through God's mercy we have this ministry. . . ."

Have you ever watched a politician on the night of his or her election—puffed up with the exaltation of victory—try to act humble? Standing before the cameras, spouse by the hand, he or she professes, "I am so humbled by this generous vote of confidence. I am undeserving, but I will do my best to earn your trust." All the time, we suspect they are really thinking, *You better believe I deserve to win this election! My opponent was an idiot, and the citizens are lucky to get a guy like me!*

The truth is, not one of us deserves the privilege of serving Christ. The Scripture makes it clear that ". . . While we were still sinners, Christ died for us" (Rom. 5:8). If we were unworthy even of salvation, how can we consider ourselves worthy of being co-workers with our Lord in the service of the kingdom?

We have this treasure, this ministry, because of God's mercy. Like our salvation itself, the call to ministry is a gift of God.

It is not a temporary call. We are called to persevere in Christ's service. There have been many suggestions for translating Paul's words in verse 1:

". . . we faint not" (KJV).

". . . we do not lose heart" (NIV).

". . . we do not play the coward" (KNOX).

". . . we do not get discouraged" (AMPLIFIED).

We are called to keep at it. When the going gets tough, keep at it! When obstacles arise, keep at it! When results seem few, keep at it! When opposition batters us, keep at it! "Since through God's mercy we have this ministry, we do not lose heart." We are called to keep at it.

Certainly it is easy to become discouraged in Christ's service. There are times when problems seem insurmountable, or when it seems that no one cares.

Charles Collins, a missionary in Guatemala, offered a discipleship class—and only one student signed up. The student prayed that his teacher would not be discouraged at being forced to prepare for only one student. The truth is, it was a bit discouraging for both teacher *and* student, but they stayed with it.

Week 13 of the study called for the student to give his testimony three times. Rather than simulate the experience, they decided to go out to find people who were without Christ. Charles remembers it this way:

> First we went to a shepherd boy tending his flock. We told him of the Good Shepherd. Then we went to a young girl cleaning in a kitchen. We told her of One who can wash us as clean as snow. Then we went to a mechanic working in a bus garage. We told him of One who can make all things new in us.
>
> The shepherd boy followed the Good Shepherd. The young girl's sins were washed away. The mechanic found One who can fix life and make it new again.[1]

When Charles asked his student if they should continue into the next portion of the course, the response was: "I think we had better finish the class. Who knows what other blessings God has in store for us?"

We have this ministry through a divine call. It is not optional, it is not deserved, it is not temporary. But it is a great treasure made available to us because of God's love and grace. Being a minister means receiving a divine call. What else characterizes the servant of God?

We Have a Trustworthy Life

As we've already seen earlier in Paul's letter, the apostle is confronting critics of his ministry who have accused him of dealing deceitfully with the Corinthian Christians. Paul is responding to those accusations by reminding his fellow believers he has conducted himself in their midst with honesty and integrity.

In verse 2, Paul asserts: "We have renounced secret and shameful ways; we do not use deception. . . ." Literally, he refers to "the hidden things of shame . . . things one may do, but will only do under cover, and with shame if found out."[2] Have you ever gone to your kitchen at night and turned on the light, only to see an insect scurry about looking for cover, trying to flee from the light? That may suggest a bit of the behavior Paul is referring to in the passage. By contrast, Paul says, he has lived his life in the open, available for all to see.

If we are to serve as effective ministers for Christ, that is the kind of life we must live—transparent, open for all to see. It is impossible to dishonor God with shameful activities, then turn around and be a useful servant of Christ in the next moment.

Paul also refers to deception; it is a word we might translate "craftiness." Hughes says the word "signifies a cunning readiness to adopt any device or trickery for the achievement of ends which are anything but altruistic."[3] Craftiness means a willingness to do whatever it takes to get the desired results; the ends justify the means, however nasty those means might be.

Sound familiar? That attitude has been splashed across the headlines of the business pages in recent years: insider trading, greenmail, and similar terms have entered our vocabulary because of this exact approach to life—I'll get *what* I want, *when* I want, any *way* I have to do it.

Lest we get too smug looking down our ecclesiastical noses at the business world, we can see the same attitude in recent years in the church. Evangelists who hire converts to stimulate a crowd; faith healers who use trickery to deceive gullible followers; preachers who use manipulative and even dishonest techniques to raise money; pastors who adopt a "chief executive officer" approach as a substitute for authentic spiritual leadership and practice whatever means are necessary to keep the "business" growing. As television villain J. R. Ewing points out, "Once integrity goes, everything else is easy."

What a tragedy when the life of a Christian becomes tarnished with dishonesty and loss of credibility. That is why Paul is so quick to defend himself in the face of such accusations. Once lost, integrity is hard to regain.

As we minister for Christ in response to a divine call, we are to have a trustworthy life. Further:

We Have an Authentic Message

One form of deception Paul had observed was a willingness to "distort the word of God . . ." (v. 2). The word translated "distort" comes from a Greek term referring to dilution of wine—adding water, for example, but selling the wine as if it were pure. Paul had in mind those who were tampering with the gospel—teaching a corrupted message—for their own purposes.

Just as in Paul's day, there are those in our time who willingly distort the gospel. How does this happen?

We can distort the gospel by increasing its demands. Paul dealt with the Judaizers, who preyed on the young Gentile Christians by insisting they must accept the ritual requirements of Judaism in order to know Christ as Savior and Lord.

Is it possible we may be guilty of just such distortion when we require adherence to our own cultural traditions as a part of Christian faith? One of the limiting factors many American missionaries faced in years past was their desire—often unconscious—to convert people to western culture and thought before bringing them to Christ.

It is easy to look at the way we "do church" as the only correct way, and in the process distort the gospel. We are called

to proclaim fully the demands of the gospel—but not add our
own expectations.

We can distort the gospel by reducing its demands. Just
as it is possible to corrupt the gospel by adding to the teaching
of Christ, so we can err on the opposite extreme.

In his first letter to this same Corinthian church, Paul was
forced to deal with moral corruption within the church—those
who acted as if Christian freedom meant they could sin at
will. In Romans 6:1, 2, Paul teaches, "Shall we go on sinning
so that grace may increase? By no means! . . ."

When we ignore God's will in favor of our own, we distort
the gospel. There is an element of obedience inherent in the
gospel; we surrender ourselves to Christ as Savior *and* Lord.
Any effort to discount the reality of Christ's Lordship in our
lives is a distortion of the gospel.

How strange, then, is the frequent teaching in our pulpits
and classrooms that surrender to Christ as Savior precedes
acceptance of Christ's Lordship. The modern dichotomy that
has been created between those experiences is simply not
found in Scripture. In the New Testament, there is no prece-
dent for men and women accepting Christ as Savior and then
later, in a deeper spiritual experience, accepting him as Lord.
Those two elements were one and the same in the New Testament. I come to Christ as Savior *and* Lord—or I do not
come at all.

Do we not grow in our commitment to Christ as time goes
on? Absolutely! Our walk with Christ matures day by day as
we know him better; and as we are shaped more and more in
his image. Yet that grows out of our commitment to Christ as
Lord of our lives.

Just as we must be careful not to add to the gospel, so we
must avoid the temptation to shortchange the demands of the
gospel, offering an "easy-believism" that does not correspond
to the teaching of the New Testament. As Paul says, "On the
contrary, by setting forth the truth plainly we commend ourselves to every man's conscience in the sight of God" (v. 2). By
living trustworthy lives and proclaiming the authentic mes-

sage of Jesus Christ, God is able to use us to minister to a lost and dying world.

There is one other characteristic Paul cites as being part of our lives as ministers of Christ:

We Have a Clear Focus

"For we do not preach ourselves," says Paul, "but Jesus Christ as Lord . . ." (v. 5). And again in verse 7: "But we have this treasure in jars of clay to show that this all-surpassing power is from God and not from us."

As servants of Christ ministering in his name, our focus is not on ourselves, our beliefs, our churches; rather, we focus clearly on the Lord Jesus. *He* is our message. *He* is our focus.

Paul's critics attacked his personal appearance and his speech, thinking they would discredit him in the churches. Yet rather than defend his appearance or other personal characteristics, Paul draws on these criticisms to emphasize that human weakness is not a limitation when God wishes to use us. "If God can use me," Paul might say, "weak and ugly as I am, then certainly God can use anyone as a minister—even you!"

That's the meaning behind the image in verse 7. Clay vessels were common in Paul's day; they were used as jars, as lamps— in many ways. They were inexpensive and plentiful, but they were also fragile and easily broken. Yet these cheap, fragile vessels could be used to store precious things.

Even today, the favorite king of the Bavarian people is "Mad" King Ludwig II, who lived in the nineteenth century. He was called "Mad" because of his eccentricities, including building a series of fantasy castles that are now popular tourist sites. (Maybe Ludwig wasn't so mad after all!)

One of the most beautiful of these castles is Schloss Linderhof. Though not very large, this castle is filled to overflowing with elaborate furnishings, beautiful art, and precious gems. In fact, there is so much packed into those few rooms that nothing in particular stands out.

If, on the other hand, a handful of those precious stones were placed by themselves in a plain wooden box, the impact would be quite different. Those gems would stand out in the midst of that simple setting.

We are like earthen vessels, Paul says, but our weakness only serves to highlight the wonder and glory of the Lord whom we serve. You and I are not the message, but the messengers; we are the vessels through which the gospel is carried to the ends of the earth. Rather than regret our weakness, we are able to rejoice that God can so wondrously use that very weakness to his glory. Our focus is on him.

Dad took lots of pictures during the family's vacation at the beach. Though family members were always in the foreground of the picture, Mom was puzzled at why so many of the pictures were fuzzy, out of focus. She finally realized, though, that in most of those photos, something *was* in focus: a bikini-clad young lady in the background. Dad had simply been focusing on the wrong subject!

It's easy to do that, isn't it? As individuals, we can focus on money, ambition, position. As churches we can focus on ceremony, on tradition, or on simply maintaining the program. Yet if we are to be effective ministers for Christ, our focus must be on Jesus alone.

What a treasure God has placed in your hands and mine—the privilege of sharing in the work of his kingdom; the privilege of leading others to faith in Christ, and nurturing them as disciples. Though we are but earthen vessels—unworthy in and of ourselves—through God's grace we can become something special.

You have the treasure. Will you use it?

7

The Coming Glory

(2 Corinthians 4:16—5:10)

Robert Ingersoll was America's best-known atheist in the nineteenth century. He traveled the country giving lectures to support his views that God did not exist.

When Ingersoll died, his brother spoke at his funeral. Among the comments were these words: "Life is a narrow vale between the cold and barren peaks of two eternities. We strive in vain to look beyond the heights. We cry aloud, and the only answer is the echo of a wailing cry."

What a note of despair! For Ingersoll and for every man or woman apart from Christ, death is the final enemy, the ultimate conqueror. Beyond death there is no hope.

For the apostle Paul the future did not hold despair and hopelessness. As he looked to the future, he saw glory and hope.

In the verses preceding this passage, Paul has recalled some of the difficulties and problems he faced in his service for Christ. Yet rather than lose heart in the face of such problems and suffering, Paul rejoices in them because they are steps along a pathway leading to a greater glory. Temporary afflictions are merely preparing him for a more wondrous glory to come.

Like Paul, as we walk with Christ, we are day by day moving toward that coming glory. For us, death need not be an approaching villain; for the Christian, death is the doorway to a greater glory in Christ Jesus. Note what Paul says about the coming glory.

The Coming Glory Is Eternal

I heard one elderly man describe how he began his day. He said he would first open the newspaper and check the obituaries. If his name wasn't listed, he'd figure it was safe to get out of bed!

The truth is, all of us are here temporarily. This life is not permanent. In 5:1, Paul calls it an "earthly tent." For a person in that day, the tent symbolized a temporary shelter; tents were used by nomadic people who were here and then gone.

With all the contemporary interest in health and fitness, you have certainly heard the warning: "Take care of your body; it's the only one you've got." That's not only true, it's also good theology! This body is the only one we've got, and it is not going to last forever no matter how well we treat it.

Yet for those who are in Christ, there is coming a day when this earthly, temporary body will be replaced by something new, something eternal. As Paul assures us in verse 1, this earthly tent will be replaced by a greater glory, "a building from God, an eternal house in heaven, not built with human hands."

One day, you and I will put off these temporary bodies and God will put on us a resurrection body. Indeed, in verse 2 Paul points out that he longs for the day when he would be clothed with this new, spiritual body—this "heavenly dwelling." Shortly after writing this letter to the Corinthians, Paul would write in his letter to the Romans: ". . . we ourselves, who have the firstfruits of the Spirit, groan inwardly as we wait eagerly for our adoption as sons, the redemption of our bodies" (Rom. 8:23).

And this new body will be eternal. ". . . For what is seen is temporary," Paul says, "but what is unseen is eternal" (4:18). Our resurrection bodies belong to the age to come. At death, we leave behind these bodies and enter into a new dimension of life with God for all eternity.

The coming glory will be eternal. Further:

The Coming Glory Is Guaranteed
by the Holy Spirit

We need not fear the future, Paul says, for God "has given us the Spirit as a deposit, guaranteeing what is to come" (5:5). When you buy a car or a house, you make a deposit—a down payment—as good faith that you will proceed with the purchase. Your deposit shows you are sincere and serious about making the transaction. Paul says God has shown his good faith toward us by placing the Holy Spirit within us. The Spirit's presence is God's assurance that we will experience the coming glory promised to all believers. As George Beasley-Murray observes, "In sending him (the Spirit) to his people, God has given the first installment of the totality of his salvation, and so a guarantee that the rest will follow."[1]

The Holy Spirit not only guarantees us of glory to come; he also gives us a taste of that glory in the present life. Already the Spirit of God is at work in the life of every believer, shaping us into the image of Christ, preparing us for the ultimate redemption of our bodies.

God wants your life *right now* to prepare you for the coming glory of life with him. In your thoughts, your actions, your attitudes, you are "in training" for the age to come.

Prior to participating in the Olympic Games, an athlete puts in thousands of hours in training and preparation—getting body and mind equipped to insure the finest possible performance in the actual event.

Suppose an endurance runner—we'll call him Bill—arrived in training camp fifty pounds overweight, carrying suitcases of junk food and gossip magazines. The first morning of training, every athlete is on the track stretching and preparing—except for Bill. Bill is still fast asleep. They go to rouse him, but Bill assures them he'll worry about training later—maybe in a week or so. You can be fairly sure that Bill will be on the next plane home, and the coach will be finding a runner who *wants* to compete and will put in the hard work required.

As disciples of Jesus Christ, we are called to run the good race, leading to the ultimate glory of life with Christ. Unless we are willing to be obedient in service now, how will the Holy Spirit shape us and prepare us for the age to come? You and I are in training for the coming glory.

The coming glory is eternal—we will be forever with the Lord. And the coming glory is guaranteed by the presence of the Holy Spirit, who is even now preparing us for that day. Paul provides us with a further truth:

The Coming Glory Involves Judgment

"For we must all appear before the judgment seat of Christ, that each one may receive what is due him for the things done while in the body, whether good or bad" (5:10).

The word used in verse 10 for judgment seat is *bema*. If you visit the ruins of ancient Corinth, you will learn that there still exists a large stone structure identified as the *bema*. It is a speaker's platform, and was used for holding trials.[2]

We read in Acts 18 that Paul was brought before the court, the *bema*, by a group of Corinthian Jews who sought the aid of the proconsul, Gallio, in silencing Paul. Gallio, however, was angry that they brought a Jewish religious matter before him, and he threw them out of the *bema*, the court.

Paul knew what it meant to stand before the judgment seat of Roman authority. Yet that was not the most impressive tribunal for Paul; instead, he knew that the most important tribunal he would ever experience would be at the *bema*, the judgment seat of Christ.

As believers, we will not stand before the judgment seat to determine our eternal destiny, for that is determined when you commit your life to Jesus Christ as Savior and Lord. Rather Paul wants us to understand that the judgment seat of Christ is where we will have our lives evaluated for what we have done, both good and bad, that we might receive reward based on faithful service—or be denied reward.

What we do in this life for Christ—or fail to do for Christ—

does have serious implications. We are accountable for our actions. Someday, we will stand before a holy and righteous Lord to answer for our lives.

What will you and I carry before the judgment seat of Christ? What faithful service will we be able to lay at his feet? What kind of life will we be able to present to the One who gave his life for us?

As I think about that day when I will stand before my Lord and he will stretch out my life before me, I wonder what kind of picture I will see. Will I have been faithful in sharing his love with others? Will I have prayed enough, cared enough, given enough of myself for his kingdom's sake? Will I have been merciful enough, forgiving enough? As the Lord Jesus looks at my Christian life, will he be able to say, "Well done, my good and faithful servant," or will my heart break as I see the tears in his precious eyes?

What can we do to prepare for that day?

First, if you have never given your life to Christ as Savior and Lord, right now give your heart and life to him. Invite him to come into your life and make it his forever.

As Christians, there is another way we must prepare for that day. Paul says in 1 Corinthians 11:31, "But if we judged ourselves, we would not come under judgment." Will you enter into the presence of God and judge yourself on those areas of your life which you know are not honoring to God? Declare that which is sinful and ask God's forgiveness and cleansing; then commit yourself to leave that sin behind.

One of the most precious promises a believer has is that "If we confess our sins, he is faithful and just to forgive us our sins and to cleanse us from all unrighteousness" (1 John 1:9). When you allow sin a place in your life, stop immediately and judge it, seeking God's forgiveness and cleansing.

How tragic to enter eternity standing ashamed before the judgment seat of Christ! But how glorious to stand before the Lord forgiven and faithful.

There is a coming glory. One day this earthly life will come to an end, and we will enter a new dimension of existence with Christ.

Charles Lindbergh was one of America's great heroes. This young adventurer who was the first to fly solo across the Atlantic Ocean, faced a final challenge later in life: cancer. Knowing that his cancer was terminal, Lindbergh and his wife moved to a vacation home in Hawaii to spend his remaining days.

Despite the illness that was cutting short his life, Lindbergh's faith in God kept him strong. He wrote the words for the minister to repeat at his burial service. They went like this:

> "We commit the body of Charles Lindbergh to its final resting place; but his spirit we commit to Almighty God, knowing that death is but a new adventure in existence. . . ."

For the one who knows Christ, death is indeed "a new adventure in existence." For the believer, there is a coming glory.

8

Why Share Christ?

(2 Corinthians 5:11–21)

Southern Baptists have come to be known in the evangelical world for their commitment to evangelism. Part of that reputation comes from well-known Southern Baptist evangelists like Billy Graham, and part from the continued rise in baptisms each year among Baptists.

Yet the Southern Baptist Home Mission Board recently reported that less than 5 percent of all Baptist church members participate in any kind of personal evangelism. That's less than one out of every twenty church members! And if one of the fastest-growing evangelical denominations is experiencing that kind of apathy in the pew concerning evangelism, where does that place many of our other denominations?

It is fair to ask ourselves the question: do we *really* believe it is important to share Christ? Are we convinced that *we* have a responsibility to reach others with the gospel?

Paul had no question about the issue of evangelism. Not only did he recognize God's call on his own life to share the gospel, he also realized God was calling every believer to a ministry of reconciliation. We are all called to share Christ.

This particular passage has been called one of the most significant in all of Paul's writings, because in it we find a summary of the essential teachings of the gospel. In these verses we find a concentrated package of the key elements of the Christian faith. And it is no accident that such a summary is set in the context of a message urging the believers to share Christ, for at the heart of our faith is the challenge and the

privilege of carrying the good news of Jesus Christ to a lost
and dying world.

Each one of us has been called by God to be a minister of
reconciliation; we are ambassadors of the Lord Jesus Christ,
carrying his message wherever we go.

We Share Christ Because We Fear God

Paul has just reminded the Corinthian believers that each
of us will stand before the judgment seat of Christ (5:10). As
he begins verse 11, he makes the transition, "Since, then, we
know what it is to fear the Lord, we try to persuade men. . . ."

We know that one day we will stand before the Lord Jesus
Christ and answer for the actions and inactions of our earthly
lives; that is enough to engender a healthy bit of fear in anyone. Paul wants us to channel that fear into a positive response: sharing Christ.

Each of us will give an account of our stewardship; we will
stand before Christ and acknowledge what we did—or failed
to do—for him. That was enough to give renewed motivation
to the apostle Paul, and he gave himself wholeheartedly in
sharing Christ with lost men and women.

If you have ever had a job working for someone, you know
what it means to be accountable for your actions. If you sell
cars or real estate, you know that unless you sell you don't
eat. If you work in an office, you have a different kind of pro-
duction, but you still must produce results or you'll be reading
the help-wanted ads pretty soon. In every area of life, there is
accountability.

Paul is saying that you and I are accountable to God for
sharing our faith. One day in the future, every one of us will
stand before the judgment seat of Christ and answer for what
we have done on behalf of the One who gave his life for us.

On that day, what will *you* say?

"Well, Lord, you see in the business world it just isn't ap-
propriate to talk about religion. It could hurt your career."

"Well, Lord, I was afraid to talk about you with the other

folks in the office. I didn't want to sound like a religious fanatic."

"Well, Lord, the other kids in school would have thought I was really stupid if I had gone around telling them about you."

"Well, Lord, I just never did get around to telling the neighbors about you. Besides, you know they were *different* from us."

"Well, Lord, I just never thought you were important enough to work into the conversation."

When we stand before God on that awesome day, he will not say, "Oh, that's all right—you didn't have to share the gospel with people who were different, with people who were poor, with people who were another color, with people who didn't talk like you or look like you." May God have mercy on us if we stand before him on that day with blood on our hands because we didn't care that men and women, boys and girls, all around us were dying and entering eternity without Christ.

Paul says, "Since, then, we know what it is to fear the Lord, we try to persuade men." Knowing that we will answer to the Lord Jesus Christ for what we say or don't say about him, we share Christ. Further:

We Share Christ Because His Love Compels Us

Fear is certainly an effective motivator, but how much greater to share Christ in response to his amazing love and in thankfulness for his grace! That is why Paul exclaims, "For Christ's love compels us . . ." (5:14).

Christ's love became the great motivator of Paul's life and work. Paul's love of Christ grew out of Christ's love for Paul, and that great love drove Paul to a life of service for his Lord. Over and over in his writings, Paul would proclaim Christ's love:

In Romans 5:8: But God demonstrates his own love for us in this: While we were still sinners, Christ died for us.

In Galatians 2:20: I have been crucified with Christ and I
no longer live, but Christ lives in me. The life I live in the body,
I live by faith in the Son of God, who loved me and gave himself
for me.

In Ephesians 3:17, 18: . . . And I pray that you, being rooted
and established in love, may have power, together with all the
saints, to grasp how wide and long and high and deep is the
love of Christ.

In *Sweet Thursday* John Steinbeck told of a young pros-
titute named Susie who was beginning a new life. In a series
of affirmations, the girl's friend said, "I am Susie and nobody
else," and Susie would repeat, "I am Susie and nobody else."
The friend said, "I am a good thing," and Susie answered, "I
am a good thing." The woman went on: "And there ain't nothing like me in the whole world."

Susie began to speak those words: "And there ain't nothing . . ."—but she suddenly stopped and burst into tears, so
overwhelmed was she at the thought that someone could know
who she was, what she was, and still love her.

That's what Jesus has done for you and me. He knows who
we are; he knows what we have done. And still he loves us;
still he gave his life for us. What a marvel that Christ would
love us so! In the words of the hymn "Love so amazing, so
divine, demands my soul, my life, my all."

Love so amazing demands a response. Paul says the love of
Christ compels us to share that love with others. Have you
responded to that great love by sharing his love with someone
else? We share Christ because of his love.

We Share Christ Because
We Have Been Called by God

"Therefore, if anyone is in Christ, he is a new creation; the
old has gone, the new has come!" (5:17).

As French L. Arrington points out: "Jesus didn't bring a
new religion but a new creation. . . . There is a great change—

a sharp reorientation of our loyalties, new hopes, new joys. There is a new lifestyle determined by the fact that we are in Christ."[1]

When you surrendered your life to Christ as Savior and Lord, something altogether new began in your life. You didn't simply add on a new element to your life; your life was transformed by the work of the Holy Spirit. You became a new creation, sharing Christ's life.

And like Christ, we have been given the ministry of reconciliation. That is what Paul tells us in verses 18 and 19:

All this is from God, who reconciled us to himself through Christ and gave us the ministry of reconciliation: that God was reconciling the world to himself in Christ, not counting men's sins against them. And he has committed to us the message of reconciliation.

Jesus Christ took on himself the sins for which we should have rightfully paid the price. He gave his own life that we might be reconciled to the Father; like the prodigal son who has "come to himself" and returned home, we have been accepted, forgiven, reconciled.

As new creatures in Christ, as citizens of the kingdom of God, we have been called to a tremendous task: we are to be ministers of that same reconciliation. That is the calling of the whole church. Every man or woman, boy or girl, who has committed his or her life to Jesus Christ has been made a minister. We are all ministers of reconciliation; to every Christian has been committed this message to share.

That is why Paul says, in verse 20, that we have been made "Christ's ambassadors, as though God were making his appeal through us. . . ." When the president of the United States appoints an ambassador to Great Britain or France or any other nation, that person is commissioned to speak on behalf of the president and the American government. He or she represents our interests and our commitments in that place.

God has called you to be his ambassador. You and I are to

be his representatives, to speak on his behalf, as ministers of God's reconciliation. To whom will the world turn to hear the words of life if Christ's followers will not proclaim them? We have been called to share Christ.

Some years ago, when many American missionaries were allowed to serve in China, a blind Chinese man was taken to a mission hospital. The missionary doctor performed an operation and removed cataracts from the man's eyes. Soon, the man was able to return to his home, rejoicing in his restored eyesight.

In a few weeks the missionaries at the hospital saw the man coming back down the road toward them—but this time he was holding a rope to which forty other blind people were clinging. He was bringing them to the place where his sight had been restored.

That is what God calls on us to do. You and I received life from the Lord Jesus Christ—life abundant, life eternal. Now it is our privilege and our calling to lead others to that same One from whom we received life. In a world filled with death and sorrow, we alone have the words of life. Do we dare to keep silent?

9

The Tragedy of Delay
(2 Corinthians 6:1–2)

I'm a channel flipper. You probably know someone like me; you may even *be* someone like me! We channel flippers get a television set with remote control so that we can flip back and forth between channels with the press of a button. I drive my wife crazy popping up and down the dial, landing on each channel for about two seconds, then flipping to the next channel in search of something worth staying with.

Recently I saw just a bit of an old movie in which just as the convicted murderer was being led to the electric chair, a witness showed up in the governor's office to testify that the convicted man was really innocent. The governor immediately took the telephone and called the warden to halt the execution, but it took a long time before anyone answered the phone.

Finally a prison officer answered the phone, and the governor barked out the order to halt the execution. But just then, the officer looked and saw the lights in the room flicker. He said to the governor, "You're too late—the execution just took place."

I don't know what happened after that, since I flipped the channel. Still, I started thinking about that scene a little later. What a terrible thing it would be for someone to be executed by mistake, simply because a witness delayed his testimony, or because a prison guard delayed answering the telephone.

The tragedy of delay. Paul knew that feeling. Many times he must have recreated in his mind's eye the scene in which he held the coats of the men who stoned Stephen for his Chris-

tian faith. Perhaps there were times when he thought to himself, *If only I had come to know Christ sooner, perhaps that
terrible tragedy might never have happened.*

In this passage, Paul warns the Corinthian church of the
danger of delay. In verse 2, he quotes from Isaiah 49:8, a passage that originally applied to the restoration of Israel following the exile in Babylon. The time of Israel's return to Palestine
to rebuild the nation was considered their "day of salvation."
God would use his power to lead his people out of captivity
and back to their homeland.

Paul says that now, in Christ, the "day of salvation" has
come in its fullness. Through Christ God has ushered in the
new age, the "acceptable time." Paul says, *"Now* is the time of
God's favor, *now* is the day of salvation" (italics added).

As part of that "day of salvation," we have been invited to
become "God's fellow workers" (v. 1). What a privilege and joy!
We have been given the opportunity to work with the Father
in his service.

In the face of that, how tragic it is to delay our response—
how tragic to "receive God's grace in vain" (v. 1). How can that
happen in our lives?

It Is Tragic to Delay
Claiming God's Grace

One of the things Paul may have been addressing in this
passage was the potential of hearing the gospel and failing to
experience it in our own lives.

In his parable of the sower, Jesus talked about just such a
possibility. In Mark 4:16–17, Jesus is explaining the parable
to his disciples, and says some who hear the gospel are "like
seed sown on rocky places, hear the word and at once receive
it with joy. But since they have no root, they last only a short
time. When trouble or persecution comes because of the word,
they quickly fall away."

It is possible to hear the gospel and respond outwardly and
not inwardly. There are those who publicly affirm Christ, join

the church, and participate in activities, but who have never truly experienced repentance of sin and a commitment of their lives to Christ as Lord and Savior.

Someone has observed that it is easier to become a church member than to join most social clubs! We do a disservice to people when we invite them to accept Christ and join a church without acknowledging the utter commitment of heart and life that he demands of us. No wonder the churches are filled with men and women whose lives show little or no evidence of a real experience with Christ. It is possible for our names to be written on the church rolls but not in the Lamb's Book of Life.

Eugene F. Suter, Jr., was a student at Yale University. While he was a student, his father died and left him an inheritance of 400 thousand dollars, but Eugene refused to accept it. The trustees of the estate, in frustration at this turn of events, took the young man to court to force him to accept the estate. The judge, however, ruled that Eugene had a legal right to refuse the bequest, and he forever cut off the young man from his family fortune.

Foolish? Most of us would think so, but how many more are there who foolishly refuse the riches of the kingdom of God, the greatest gift one could possibly receive. What a tragedy to delay knowing Christ!

Bruce Thielemann is pastor of Pittsburgh's First Presbyterian Church. He tells the story of the meeting Satan called of all his emissaries. He was looking for one demon to send to earth to help men and women destroy their own souls.

To the first volunteer, Satan posed this question: "If I send you, what will you tell the children of men?" He replied, "I will tell the children of men there is no heaven."

Satan said, "They will not believe you, for there is a bit of heaven in every human heart. In the end they know that right and good must prevail. You are not the one."

Another demon, fouler than the first, stepped forward to volunteer and Satan posed to him the same question.

"I will tell them there is no hell."

Satan responded: "They will not believe you either. For in every human heart is a conscience, an inner voice that testifies that not only will good be triumphant but evil will be defeated. You are not the one."

One last demon stepped forward to volunteer. Satan said, "What will you say to people to aid them in the destruction of their souls?"

The demon responded, "I will tell them there is no hurry."

And Satan immediately said, "You are the one. Go!"[1]

That is one of the greatest dangers of all—to think that there is no hurry, that we can delay a decision. If you have never responded to Jesus Christ in repentance and faith and commitment of your life, there is no time to delay! He calls you today. "Now is the time of God's favor, now is the day of salvation."

There is another tragedy that threatens us.

It Is Tragic to Delay
Living in God's Grace

There is another sense in which one can "receive God's grace in vain." That is when we allow our practice to fall behind our profession; when we live lives inconsistent with the will of God. When we fail to be obedient to Christ's commands, we deny the power of the gospel in our own lives.

Imagine the scene: it is dawn, the morning of the great battle. The general begins to issue orders to the troops—where they are to be on the field, the strategy they are to use, the timing of the attack. Then he begins to hear the responses from each company: "We're not feeling well this morning, so we'd better stay in." "We've got some family coming to visit, so we'd better pass on this morning's battle." "We don't like this part of the battlefield; we're going to do our fighting over there." "We're getting a little tired of this general; we want to hire another general that will be more entertaining." "The general hasn't visited us in weeks, and hasn't said one word of appreciation for the way we fought in last year's battle, so we aren't going to fight for *him* anymore!"

Sound absurd? Any army with soldiers like that would be no match for a strong, disciplined opponent. Any wonder then that the church so often refuses to win the victories that are possible, when the ranks are so full of disobedience and disinterest. Perhaps we should rewrite the words of the song to read: "Onward, Christian soldiers—unless you are tired, or have something else to do, or don't want to get involved, or have a better idea, or just really don't care!"

When our lives are inconsistent with our words, the cause of Christ suffers. When we sing, "I'll go where you want me to go, dear Lord," but aren't willing to cross the street to serve Christ, the world sees and understands all too well. What a tragedy when we refuse to allow Christ to be seen in our lives.

What does God want to do in your life? What challenge is he calling you to face? What task does he ask you to complete? What service does he give you to perform?

Do you dare to delay in responding to his call? Do you dare delay in being obedient to your Lord? "Now is the time of God's favor, now is the day of salvation."

There is still further tragedy that may face us.

It Is Tragic to Delay Sharing God's Grace

We have not been saved in order to keep it a secret. Jesus said in the Sermon on the Mount: "Neither do people light a lamp and put it under a bowl. Instead, they put it on its stand, and it gives light to everyone in the house. In the same way, let your light shine before men . . ." (Matt. 5:15, 16).

As children we sang, "This little light of mine, I'm gonna let it shine." Yet too many Christians have delayed letting their light shine before the world; we have delayed telling others about the Lord who gave us life.

How tragic that the world waits to hear the words of life while we spend our hours discussing everything but how to

reach them. All around us people hunger to know that someone cares, that someone loves them—and we remain silent.

One Buddhist monk was quoted as saying, "To the Eastern
religions it looks as if Christianity has reached the stage in
adolescence when the child is slightly ashamed of his father
and embarrassed when talking about him."

What a tragedy when the world sees our hesitancy to share
Christ and assumes we are embarrassed of him. And what a
greater tragedy when it is true!

We dare not delay in sharing Christ. Each day thousands
of children are born into our world, and as many as a third
of them may live and die without hearing the gospel. But don't
think that only happens in faraway countries. Within walking
distance of your church—or any church in any city in America—that is just as true.

Will we make that our commitment as Christians and as
a church—that the uppermost priority of our church will be
to share Christ? Will we say as the church of the Lord Jesus
Christ that nothing will be more important: not the building,
not the programs, not our comfort or preferences? Nothing
will be more important than sharing Christ with a lost and
dying world.

That's why the early Christians turned the world upside
down. There was an urgency to their service—a realization
that the time was short, that they must spread the gospel to
as many people as possible as quickly as possible. May God
help us to rekindle that kind of urgency in our day and in our
church.

Ronald Reagan told a story about his observation of the
pilots who flew Air Force One. Whenever they landed, he noticed that they touched down just as close to the end of the
runway as possible.

One day he asked one of the pilots: "With all that runway
to use, why do you work so hard to try to land right at the
beginning of the runway?"

The pilot answered: "Sir, one of the first things pilots learn
is you can't use the runway behind you!"

Perhaps the lesson we as Christians need to use is you can't use the time that's already gone by. We only have left the limited time that's ahead of us. How tragic to delay accepting Christ—to delay serving Christ—to delay sharing Christ.

God help us to redeem the time, for it is short.

10

Confidence in Ministry

(2 Corinthians 6:3–10)

The criminal burst into an Old West saloon with his guns blazing, yelling, "All you filthy skunks get out of here!"

The saloon quickly emptied as the customers ran through doors and jumped through windows—all except one Englishman, who calmly stood at the bar sipping his drink.

"Well?" said the gunman.

The Englishman responded, "Well, there certainly were a lot of them, weren't there?"

There was a man who knew what he wasn't!

Confidence is a widely appreciated quality in our day. Businesspeople spend millions attending seminars, buying books and tapes, all to gain self-confidence. From Dale Carnegie courses to assertiveness training, we are committed to gaining the extra measure of confidence that gives us the edge in business and professional life.

It is every bit as important to have confidence in ministry. If we approach our service for the Lord Jesus Christ with a sense of timidity and uncertainty, the world may well interpret that as uncertainty about the message we profess and proclaim. As servants of the King of kings—heirs of God and joint heirs of Christ—we ought to exhibit confidence in ministry.

Paul was a confident minister of Christ. He was certainly not arrogant; over and over, he reminds his fellow believers that he was undeserving of God's grace. Yet Paul served Christ with an unmistakable boldness—a triumphant confidence.

At the begining of this passage, Paul reminds the Corinthian believers that his ministry has offered no basis for dis-
crediting the work of Christ. The word used at the end of
verse 3—translated to "discredit" or "blame"—suggests the
idea of mocking or ridicule. Paul is saying his ministry has
done nothing to make a laughingstock of the church or the
gospel. What a tragedy that such cannot be said of every ministry!
We live in an era when the media seizes on news of a television
preacher who falls into sin, or a minister who steals from his
flock—and immediately every minister and every congregation is called into question. How we grieved as the work of
evangelism has been ridiculed in editorial cartoons and other
media. What a difficult lesson that has provided for every pastor and every minister.

Paul says his ministry has not been a source of embar-
rassment for the church, but rather a source of strength and
encouragement. He has not discouraged people from responding to the gospel, but has been a positive witness for Christ.

What were the characteristics of Paul's ministry which allowed him to serve with such confidence? And what elements
will help us to share that boldness in our own service for
Christ?

Endurance Produces
Confidence in Ministry

The Greek word which is here translated "endurance" is a
New Testament term with a rich meaning.

For the Greek world of Paul's day, the word came to refer to
a courageous quality that persevered by actively defying evil.
Aristotle praises the man who bravely resists evil in the face
of opposition, and this is the word he uses.[1]

As the New Testament picks up the word, the Christian
believer is to exhibit endurance, to stand fast in the face of
life's challenges, to persevere despite the difficulties of life. In
verses 4 and 5, the word *endurance* forms a broad principle

under which Paul cites specific examples in his own life—
various trials that Paul had faced in his ministry.

The list of nine falls into three groups: "troubles, hardships
and distresses" were the general circumstances in which Paul's
ministry was often carried out; "beatings, imprisonments and
riots" were external challenges Paul faced, inflicted on him by
those who opposed his ministry; "hard work, sleepless nights
and hunger" were voluntary hardships Paul willingly accepted
in order to advance Christ's cause.

Though few Western Christians in the twentieth century
have undergone the kind of brutal opposition Paul faced
(though some Christians in other parts of the world have), we
are still called to endurance.

Perhaps one of the greatest dangers we face as Christians
is the lack of overt opposition. It is easy to slip into a com-
fortable accommodation with the culture around us and allow
society to dilute the gospel; the world will gladly ignore the
radical demands of Jesus Christ and put in their place a ge-
neric, sentimental, cultural Christianity that won't offend
anyone.

The problem is that whenever we boldly proclaim the authentic gospel of Jesus Christ, it *will* offend. Jesus identified
himself as a "stumbling block" for those who refused his message. When we are true to his message, we will most certainly
encounter opposition.

It will likely be more subtle than the kind of opposition Paul
faced, but no less real. We may sacrifice social position and
status; we will face opponents who seek to exploit others for
their own gain; we will even encounter resistance from within
the church, from those for whom the gospel is more Sunday
ceremony than daily walk.

A Methodist minister from Uganda was visiting the USA,
relating the experiences of the Christian churches under the
violent persecution of Idi Amin. Thousands of Ugandan Christians literally gave their lives for their faith during those tragic
years, yet the number of Christians in Uganda was larger at
the end of Amin's reign of terror than at the beginning.

One American commented, "It must have been very difficult to be a Christian in Uganda." The minister responded, "I think it would be more difficult to be a Christian in Des Moines." An insightful comment! The opposition we face is often subtle; we may not even recognize the challenges to our faith that are being posed day by day. Yet the danger is real, and we are called to endurance.

Because Paul had faithfully endured the trials that came his way, God was able to produce within him a holy confidence. Through boldness born of endurance, Paul could proclaim, "In all these things we are more than conquerors through him that loved us" (Rom. 8:37).

Endurance produces confidence in ministry. Further:

Character Produces Confidence in Ministry

Paul's confidence in ministry did not simply grow out of his endurance; it also emerged from a Christ-like character.

Notice the elements, listed in verses 6 and 7, that worked together to compose Paul's character.

Purity. As Paul begins to list a series of spiritual qualities which God has produced in his life and which have enabled him to have this confidence in ministry, the first quality he mentions is purity.

The word Paul uses for *purity* is a term the Greeks defined as "the careful avoidance of all sins which are against the gods."[2] It is a word which expresses a life set at a higher level—a life which seeks to honor God and avoids the stain of sin.

It is common today for individual investors to purchase gold, silver, or other precious metals. When you go to purchase gold, one of the things you will insist on is a verification that the gold is pure—that it has not been mixed with other metals. Why does that matter? It matters because mixing the gold with other elements reduces its value; a bar composed of 60 percent gold and 40 percent lead is less valuable than a

bar containing 100 percent gold. Impurity reduces the value
of the metal.

The same thing is true in the Christian life. Impurity reduces our effectiveness as ministers of Christ. If we allow our
lives to be tainted with continuing sin and impurity, we will
not be the kind of servants God uses to share his love and
righteousness with a lost world. An impure life is not one that
can minister with confidence.

When Paul thought of purity, perhaps his mind's eye carried him to the workshop of the refiner. The refiner would
take gold that was mixed with other metals and he would
refine it down to its purest form. The refiner's fire produced
purity.

So often God must allow the fire of trials and difficulties to
come our way in order that we will be refined and purified.
Paul's trials and afflictions had produced not only endurance,
but also purity of life and character. Purity gives confidence
in ministry.

Understanding. The word used here, understanding or
knowledge, has been translated in many different ways: "insight"; "enlightened"; "grasp of truth." Perhaps we could best
understand it as comprehending the things of God as revealed
in Jesus Christ.

Imagine a classroom in which the teacher enters the first
day and says to the class: "Boys and girls, this is a mathematics class and I am your teacher. Unfortunately, I do not
know anything about mathematics. Therefore, I am going to
sit here at the desk and smile, while you read your textbooks
and try to learn something about math." You can just imagine
how much more difficult it would be for those students to
learn math as compared to students with a competent teacher.

How much more vital it is that we who call ourselves disciples of Jesus Christ have an understanding of the Word of
God, so that we can be adequate guides for those who don't
know Christ as Savior and Lord. To be confident in ministry,
we must spend the time with God's Word to have that understanding, that knowledge of the things of God which will make
us effective servants of Christ.

Patience. The word *patience* may also be translated as "forbearance" or "long-suffering." It represents that spiritual quality which enables us to endure ill-treatment or suffering without seeking to strike back in revenge. Some commentators believe that Paul is actually referring to patience *between Christians* in this passage.

Perhaps one of the greatest needs in the church is patience—forbearance toward one another. Certainly each of us has experienced a time when we have been offended or hurt by another Christian—sometimes intentionally, sometimes through misunderstanding. It is so easy to allow pride and hurt to mingle and produce a powerful urge to get back, to get revenge.

How much damage has been done to the cause of Christ by just such retaliation? Paul says that confidence in ministry grows out of Christ-like character, and character requires patience toward those who would do me evil.

Was there ever a greater example of this kind of patience than the example of Jesus Christ on the cross? Suspended over Calvary, suffering unjustly, as the hymn writer said, "He could have called ten thousand angels" to vindicate him and destroy his accusers. Instead, he prayed, "Father, forgive them." There is our model, if we would have Christ-like character and confidence in ministry.

Kindness. One of the first verses most of us learned as small children in Sunday school was "be ye kind one to another." What a simple reminder of such a powerful principle! Kindness is an essential part of Christian character.

All of the church activities and religious ceremonies we can perform in a lifetime are no substitute for the kind words and deeds we offer to others. The world may perceive Christ's presence in us far more through a kind act or an encouraging word than through all the sermons we preach or lessons we teach. As Henry Drummond observed, "The greatest thing a man can do for his heavenly Father is to be kind to some of his other children."

Sincere love. As he lists these spiritual qualities, Paul interjects the source of all such graces: the Holy Spirit. Then he continues the list with one of the most vital of all the qualities that produce character: *sincere love.*

Our age has produced no shortages of talk about love. We sing about love, talk about love, write about love. Turn on the television and in a matter of moments you'll hear about love: love that new car, love my cat, love my carpet. The soap operas, movies, pop music are all concerned with "love."

Yet the world has experienced very little of the kind of love Paul refers to here, for this is an unhypocritical love; a love without sham or falsehood. Paul says Christian character is reflected in a sincere, genuine love toward others.

The problem is, love is easier to talk about than to do. A psychology professor, who was himself childless, often corrected his neighbors when he saw them scolding their children. "You should love the boy, not punish him," he would urge.

One hot, summer day, the professor had been hard at work all day repairing his concrete driveway. The job finally complete, he wiped the sweat from his brow and headed toward the house for a cold drink when, out of the corner of his eye, he spied a neighborhood boy putting his hand into the fresh cement.

Rushing over and grabbing the boy, the professor was about to spank him when the next-door neighbor stepped onto the porch and said, "Professor, shouldn't you love the boy instead of punishing him?"

The professor replied, "I do love him in the abstract, but not in the concrete!"

It's easy to love folks in the abstract; it's harder to love them in the concrete. Love means attaching great value to people. It requires taking an interest in people, seeking their good, giving of oneself for their sake. That kind of love is certainly not easy—it took Jesus to Calvary's cross. In fact it is only as we allow his love to fill and direct our lives that we can truly express that kind of sincere, genuine love for others.

Paul's life exhibited these spiritual qualities—purity, understanding, patience, kindness, sincere love—as a reflection of the Christ-like character the Holy Spirit was producing in him. Character and endurance produce confidence in ministry, but there is one more vital element if we are to be all that God wants us to be as ministers of Christ.

The Power of God Produces Confidence

All of these spiritual qualities, all of the endurance Paul had developed, were useless without the presence and power of the Lord in his life. It is the power of God that activates and empowers the confidence we need to minister boldly in Christ's name.

The Corinthians had seen that power in their midst: in the endurance Paul showed toward great adversity; in the Christ-like character he displayed toward them; in the truth of the gospel he had preached to them, and by which they had come to know Christ's love and grace. They knew God's power because they had experienced it in their own lives.

Have you experienced God's power in your life? Have you allowed Christ to enter your life and produce the kind of endurance and character he wants to give you? Have you claimed his power to make you a bold, confident minister of Christ?

A Phantom fighter jet is an intimidating piece of equipment. It has tremendous power for speed and incredible firepower. Under the control of a skilled pilot, it is an awesome piece of military machinery.

But so long as the plane stays in the hangar, it is useless. It accomplishes nothing until the pilot assumes control and takes it from the hangar and into the sky. The power is there, but it must be used.

The power of God is available to make us confident, effective ministers of the Lord Jesus Christ. All that is waiting is our willingness to let God use us. Will you claim his power in your life today? Will you let him produce in you a new confidence in ministry?

11

Joy in Ministry
(2 Corinthians 7:2-7)

What brings joy to your life?

Most of us can probably think of some special moments in life that make us joyful: seeing a baby laugh; being reunited with a beloved friend; gathering around the table with friends and family on Christmas or Thanksgiving.

Despite the incredible array of trials and difficulties he underwent, the apostle Paul was a man who knew great joy. Even in the letters he wrote while imprisoned, there is a distinctive note of joy to be found. In a day when people plunge into clinical depression when the cable TV goes on the blink, it is fair to wonder how Paul was able to remain joyful in the midst of such adversity.

In this passage Paul returns to a thought begun earlier in his letter. His previous visit to Corinth had been nothing short of disastrous; it was greatly disturbing both to Paul and to the church. Because of this conflict, Paul avoided an immediate return visit; instead, he sent Titus to deliver a fairly stern letter of rebuke and correction.

Paul has gone to Macedonia to await Titus and learn of the Corinthians' response to his letter. When Titus arrives, Paul learns that the believers in Corinth received the letter positively and they look forward to Paul's return to their church—the division is over, the breach is healed.

In verse 4, Paul expresses his absolute delight with this news. He is filled with joy. In fact, the word used for *joy* is an emphatic form which we might translate: "I superabound with joy."[1]

In these verses we find the sources of Paul's joy—those elements that allowed him to be consumed with joy in the midst of affliction.

A Clear Conscience

One of the most vital characteristics Paul possessed which allowed him to have such joy was *a clear conscience.*

In verse 2, Paul reminds the Corinthian believers that ". . . we have wronged no one, we have corrupted no one, we have exploited no one." Although he had been criticized by opponents, Paul could wholeheartedly seek a place in their hearts because he came to them with a clear conscience. That is a wonderful source of joy.

He could say *we have wronged no one.* The Corinthian believers knew Paul had dealt with all of them justly. He had done nothing among them to call his integrity or good faith into question.

Lottie Moon served for nearly forty years as a Southern Baptist missionary in China. She literally gave herself in service to the people of China. When famine brought much suffering to China, Lottie Moon did without food herself, so that the people could have more to eat. When her friends and colleagues finally carried Miss Moon from her mission post to return home to the USA, she was literally starving to death; in this weakened state, she died on Christmas Eve 1912, while her ship was harbored in Japan.

Lottie Moon gave herself in sacrificial service to the people of China. Is it any wonder that she was so beloved by the people with whom she worked—and why she has become the symbol of foreign missions for Southern Baptists?

Paul could say much the same to the church at Corinth. He had given himself to them in faithful service. He had done nothing to hurt them. He had wronged no one.

Paul also said *we have corrupted no one.* There were those

who opposed Paul's teachings; they insisted that his emphasis on Christian freedom was actually a license to sin. "He is
corrupting the morals of the people," they might have argued.

Yet nothing could be further from the truth, as Paul reminded the believers in Corinth. Over and over, he had emphasized the ethical demands of the gospel—that Christian
freedom was a freedom to live for Christ, not a freedom to sin.
Paul knew there was no substance to the charges against him.
He had a clear conscience. He had corrupted no one.

Paul also reminds them that *we have exploited no one.*
That word *exploit* was a Greek term for defrauding someone,
for being guilty of dishonest financial dealings. Here was another of the charges his opponents had leveled against the
apostle—that he was a charlatan, trying to separate the church
from its money.

This is a common accusation of the church and its ministers. Whenever there is an emphasis on stewardship, there
are those who cry out, "All they ever do is talk about money!
All they want is my money!" And fuel is added to the fire
when some minister gets caught in financial impropriety; the
Elmer-Gantry-types are few, but they do exist.

In Paul's case, however, he could ridicule such assertions.
He had been so concerned about such matters that he had
refused to accept financial support from the Corinthians, even
for his own needs while working among them. As he will point
out in 12:16, he was not, nor would he be, a financial burden
to them. In fact he makes jokes: "crafty fellow that I am, I
caught you by trickery" by refusing to accept your financial
support. The only gifts he has collected from the Corinthian
church were for the poor in Jerusalem.

It is absolutely essential for ministers and for the church
to maintain a clear conscience in the realm of finances. It is
too easy to see a ministry ruined by carelessness in this area.
One of the strengths of Billy Graham's ministry—and one
reason it has continued to be so widely respected over the
years—is his emphasis on integrity in financial matters. Although he could have reaped huge personal financial rewards,

he put himself on a salary and insisted that all financial matters be handled properly. Like Paul, Billy Graham knows the value of a clear conscience in the area of money.

Paul had great joy in ministry, and one reason was that he served Christ with a clear conscience.

A Consistent Commitment

There was a second factor that contributed to Paul's joy in ministry: he had *a consistent commitment.*

So great is Paul's commitment to his flock that he could say: "you have such a place in our hearts that we would live or die with you" (v. 3). Paul has shown again and again his willingness to give himself for their sakes, even to the point of death. So great is his commitment to them that nothing can break it, in life or in death.

Few things in life bring more joy than a consistent commitment to an important cause. Perhaps you have heard of Mel Fisher. For years Fisher dreamed of discovering sunken treasure off the Florida Keys. He raised money from friends, used his own resources, and spent sixteen years chasing the dream. Though he had long since exhausted the patience of his investors and the limits of his own finances, Mel Fisher clung to the commitment he had made—and in August of 1985 the dream became reality as his team discovered silver ingots estimated in value at over $400 million. What was Mel Fisher's reaction? Not surprising: he shouted with joy!

Paul had a consistent commitment to God's call in his life, and the result was a deep-rooted joy. Is there a consistent commitment in your life? Have you allowed God to place upon your heart and life a special task, a dynamic calling? It is in that kind of commitment that you and I find the greatest joy in life—for it is there we find God's abiding presence.

Paul's joy grew out of a clear conscience and a consistent commitment. In this passage we find yet another source of joy.

A Comforting Colleague

One of the greatest sources of joy Paul cites in these verses is the arrival of *a comforting colleague*, Titus. Note Paul's statement in verses 6 and 7: "But God, who comforts the downcast, comforted us by the coming of Titus, and not only by his coming but also by the comfort you had given him. He told us about your longing for me, your deep sorrow, your ardent concern for me, so that my joy was greater than ever."

There were two factors here that brought joy to Paul's heart:

1. *The return of a friend.* Titus was a beloved co-worker of Paul. Though we know his name from the letter Paul wrote to him, now part of our New Testament, few Christians know much about Titus.

He was a Gentile who accompanied Paul and Barnabas to Jerusalem during the controversy over how Gentiles might become Christians. He apparently accompanied Paul on other missionary journeys; some have suggested his name was not listed in the Book of Acts because he may have been the brother of Luke, who wrote Acts.

Titus must have been well trusted by Paul, for it was Titus who was given the delicate and important task of helping ease the relationship between Paul and the Corinthian church. Later Paul would send Titus on other key evangelistic missions, and tradition says that he spent the last years of his life as a bishop in Crete.

So when Paul receives Titus in Macedonia, carrying news of the trip to Corinth, Paul is receiving one who has been friend, colleague, a beloved brother in Christ. The arrival of Titus brings joy to Paul's heart.

There are few blessings of God greater than true friends. We know joy in the presence of those whose hearts are made one with us in friendship, for they bring support, counsel, encouragement, insight. As Robert South said, "A true friend is the gift of God, and he only who made hearts can unite them."

Do you have a friend like that? Are *you* a friend like that? The most certain way of having such a friend is by offering ourselves as such a friend.

The return of a friend brought joy to Paul. Something else which gave Paul great joy was:

2. *The reconciliation with brothers and sisters in Christ.* Titus had carried a severe letter of correction from Paul to Corinth, and the apostle had been concerned about the kind of response Titus would receive from the church.

Upon Titus' return Paul was filled with joy to learn that the Corinthian church had received Titus warmly and had responded to Paul's letter with repentance and renewed commitment. Indeed, they sent word of their love and concern for Paul, and their desire that he return to them personally. Paul was overjoyed at news of this wonderful reconciliation with a group of Christian brothers and sisters.

Division among Christians is always tragic. We bring dishonor to the name of our Lord when we engage in bickering and conflict within the Body of Christ.

On the other hand, reconciliation between Christians brings great joy and new effectiveness in ministry.

A parable is told of what heaven and hell are like. In hell, they say, everyone is seated around a giant table upon which is set a magnificent feast. The problem is, each person's arm is fixed in a straight position; no elbows will bend. As a result, there is terrible frustration for all eternity as hell's inhabitants try unsuccessfully to feed themselves.

In heaven, they say, the same table is set with the same magnificent feast. Likewise, arms are straight; no elbows will bend. But in heaven, there is great joy because God's children feed one another.

That's what God has in mind for *his* children—not just in eternity but also in this present age. How much more we could see accomplished for the kingdom if we would lay aside strife and rivalries and bitterness, and be reconciled one to another. We will know Paul's joy when we too are reconciled to one another as brothers and sisters in Christ.

Joy in ministry becomes a reality in our lives when we yield our lives to his control—when we place ourselves in the hands of the One who is the Creator and sustainer of all joy.

12

When Bad News Becomes Good News

(2 Corinthians 7:8–12)

I heard about a man who received a telephone call, and on the other end of the line heard a voice saying: "I've got some good news and some bad news. Your mother-in-law just drove your brand-new Cadillac over a cliff."

With apologies to all mothers-in-law, you get the idea. You've probably heard a hundred jokes with the opening phrase, "I've got some good news and some bad news. . . ." It does strike a note of reality for us, since life is full of news that contains both good and bad.

Paul had already received the bad news. He dearly loved the church at Corinth, and he was distressed to learn of the turmoil and problems that had engulfed that congregation. In fact, in response to the situation he dispatched his colleague Titus to deliver a severe letter of correction to the Corinthian believers. Some scholars believe the letter of First Corinthians was the epistle to which Paul refers here; more believe that the "severe letter" was an altogether different—even sterner—letter which was subsequently lost to history.

Whatever was the nature of that severe letter, since sending it Paul had been worried about the response Titus would receive in Corinth and how the church would react to Paul's challenge. Paul had many sleepless nights (7:5) as he wrestled with his concern for the Corinthian church. As he says in verse 8, there was even a point at which he regretted having sent the severe letter, for fear that the church would react badly and that a further breach might develop between himself and the believers there.

Now Titus has returned to Paul with wonderful news: not only did the Corinthian church receive him with warm hospitality, they also responded to Paul's letter with an outpouring of repentance and concern. The bad news has become good news.

There are times in the life of every Christian and every church when we need to be confronted. We need leaders and friends who will deal forthrightly with the problem—whatever that may be—and challenge us to change. This passage provides a model that helps us understand how bad news can become good news in our lives.

A Challenge Can Lead to Sorrow

Although Paul momentarily regretted his sending of the severe letter, now he was glad he had challenged the Corinthian believers, for this challenge had led them to sorrow for sin. They felt remorse for what they had done—for the corruption they had allowed to enter their midst, and for the suspicions about Paul they had allowed to be planted by false teachers.

Sorrow for sin is an essential stepping-stone to correction and restoration. Unless we are convicted of the wrongness of our actions and feel a sense of sorrow or remorse, there is little motivation for us to walk a different path. As Lord Byron observed, "Sorrow is knowledge; they who know the most must mourn the deepest o'er the fatal truth."

Yet sorrow alone is not adequate. Judas was sorrowful, remorseful, over the results of his actions, but it did not produce a changed life. Something more is needed.

Sorrow Must Lead to Repentance

Sorrow and repentance are two different things. The Greek word Paul uses in verse 9 for sorrow is *lupe*, which expresses regret or remorse. He goes on to say in that same verse, "Yet now I am happy, not because you were made sorry, but because your sorrow led you to repentance. . . ."

The word "repentance" is *metanoia*. That word is based on a Greek root that meant "to have a change of heart toward something." In the New Testament, the word is used to express a turning from sin and toward God. As A. T. Robertson points out, "It was not mere sorrow, but a change in their attitude that counted."[1]

For Paul the sorrow they felt was a necessary prelude to the repentance they experienced—but sorrow for sin without authentic repentance is inadequate. Simple remorse for sin, without repentance, is like furiously bailing the water from a canoe while failing to cover the two-foot hole in the bottom of the craft; no matter how fast we bail, there will always be more water coming in than going out. Sorrow must lead *to* repentance.

In verse 10, Paul indicates that, "Godly sorrow brings repentance that leads to salvation and leaves no regret, but worldly sorrow brings death." What is the difference between "godly sorrow" and "worldly sorrow"?

Godly sorrow is divinely inspired, while worldly sorrow is humanly inspired. The Holy Spirit works in the life of an individual to bring about godly sorrow. Worldly sorrow, on the other hand, is inspired by the consequences of our actions or attitudes. Worldly sorrow does not grow out of distaste for sin, but out of distress at the *painful consequences of sin.* Godly sorrow is directed toward God; worldly sorrow is focused on self.

Godly sorrow results in repentance, while worldly sorrow results in remorse. Godly sorrow involves regret for sin and a turning to God in repentance and faith. Worldly sorrow, on the other hand, goes no further than remorse. It involves regret over what has happened—the consequences of sin—but there is no change of heart, no change of attitude, no change of life.

Esau sold his birthright for a meal, and afterward bitterly

regretted what he had done. He was sorrowful for his past
mistake, even to the point of tears, but as Hebrews 12:17
points out, "He could bring about no change of mind." There
was worldly sorrow but no repentance.

Providing a sharp contrast to Esau is another Old Testament character, David. David also sinned, committing adultery with Bathsheba and having her husband killed in battle.
When confronted with his sin, however, David was filled
with sorrow, and that sorrow led to sincere repentance. He
confessed:

Wash away all my iniquity
   and cleanse me from my sin.
For I know my transgressions,
   and my sin is always before me.
Against you, you only, have I sinned
   and done what is evil in your sight" (Ps. 51:2–4).

David experienced godly sorrow, and it resulted in a repentant
heart and life.

*Godly sorrow results in victory, while worldly sorrow ends
in defeat.* Godly sorrow produces repentance, and restores
our relationship with God. Following his prayer of confession
and repentance, David could exclaim, "Restore to me the joy
of your salvation . . ." (Ps. 51:12).

Worldly sorrow, on the other hand, produces no victory—
only frustration, emptiness, defeat. Judas felt sorrow for
his betrayal of Christ, but there was no victory—only a pa-
thetic suicide. Sorrow apart from repentance is ultimately
meaningless.

Paul rejoiced that his beloved church in Corinth had experienced sincere repentance, for:

Repentance Leads to Salvation

Apart from sincere repentance, there is no salvation. At the
very beginning of his public ministry, Jesus said, "Repent, for

the kingdom of heaven is near" (Matt. 4:17). At the end of his ministry and just prior to his ascension, Jesus said, ". . . This is what is written: The Christ will suffer and rise from the dead on the third day, and repentance and forgiveness of sins will be preached in his name to all nations" (Luke 24:45).

On the day of Pentecost, as the Holy Spirit came upon the early Christians and empowered them for service, Peter presented the first gospel sermon. What was at the heart of his message? "Repent and be baptized, every one of you, in the name of Jesus Christ so that your sins may be forgiven . . ." (Acts 2:38). Repentance of sin—turning away from the old life and turning toward a new life with Christ—is absolutely essential to salvation.

There are few more vivid examples of repentance than Zacchaeus the tax collector. Here was a man who had abused his position to line his own pockets—not an uncommon practice among tax collectors in those days. When Jesus came to Jericho, curiosity sent Zacchaeus climbing a tree to see the popular preacher as he passed by.

Yet when Jesus reached out to Zacchaeus in love and concern, a miracle of repentance took place in the man's life. One who had spent his life exploiting others for financial gain did a complete reversal, promising to give half his possessions to the poor and to repay all those he had cheated the amount owed times four (Luke 19:1–10). What happened to cause such a change? Zacchaeus was convicted of sin and repented.

Unless repentance takes place—a change of heart, a change of life, a turning toward God—there is no salvation.

Dr. Maltie D. Babcock was a Presbyterian pastor in Brooklyn, New York. In his day, it was common for churches to rent pews to members as a source of financial support, but Babcock brought an end to the practice in his church and opened the pews to the public.

One wealthy woman—a long-time member of the church—was furious at this change. The first Sunday that she entered the sanctuary and found strangers in "her" pew, she stamped out and pledged she would never again speak a word to the pastor.

Dr. Babcock quickly heard about the problem, and on Monday sought to reconcile with her by visiting in her home. The maid came to the door and announced, "The lady of the house is not at home." The pastor returned on Tuesday and received the same greeting: "The lady of the house is not at home." The scene was repeated on Wednesday and Thursday.

That last day, however, Babcock adopted a new strategy. Before the maid could stop him, he put his foot in the door and said to her, "Please tell the lady of the house that her pastor is waiting for her in the parlor."

The disgruntled member was in another area of the house with her husband and two daughters, and was beside herself to hear that the pushy preacher had invaded her home. One of the daughters said, "Calm down, mother. I'll go to the parlor and escort him out of the house."

She entered the parlor, unaware of the pastor's winsome appeal. He quickly had the daughter involved in a conversation about her own need for Christ. In a few minutes, she had prayed and asked Christ to become her Lord and Savior.

When the first daughter failed to reappear, the mother sent the second girl down to see what was happening. Upon entering the parlor, the second daughter was surprised to see the expression on her sister's face. Immediately, Dr. Babcock began explaining to this young lady about the change that had taken place in her sister's life. Soon she also gave her heart to Christ.

By then it was too much for the mother to bear. Carrying a load of bitterness, she strode into the parlor to dispatch the insolent pastor. When she saw Babcock, however, she was taken aback to see him standing with her two daughters, both looking more radiant than they had ever looked.

"Madam, your two precious daughters have just accepted Christ as their Lord and Savior. We were just about to kneel and pray together. Won't you come join us and give yourself to the Lord anew?"

The woman—who moments before had been filled with anger—now was consumed with conviction of sin and repentance. As God's Spirit touched her life, she confessed, "Pastor, what is a church pew to compare with my daughters' knowing Christ!" That day a family was united in the Lord through repentance and fresh commitment to Christ.

Paul appealed to the believers at Corinth to repent and be restored. That same appeal is open to you today—to come to Christ in godly sorrow and repentance, to experience forgiveness of sins, to receive his salvation.

As the apostle wrote, "Godly sorrow brings repentance that leads to salvation," and once that commitment is made, "it leaves no regret" (v. 10).

13

What Real Giving Means
(2 Corinthians 8:1–12)

They call it "Black Monday." On October 19, 1987, the New York Stock Exchange experienced a 508-point drop in the Dow Jones Industrial Average. Of course that simply brought the Dow Jones average back to where it stood at the end of 1986, but to hear the media analysts describe it you'd arrive at the conclusion that the world had come to an end that day.

It is amazing how much of an impact money has on our lives. It touches every area of life: career, family, leisure. It also touches our spiritual lives.

Paul knew that. He was writing to the church at Corinth about their role in a special offering he was gathering for the church in Jerusalem. Like most religious centers, Jerusalem attracted many of the poor and destitute of the land. Many of these poor people in Jerusalem were coming to faith in Christ, joining other Christians who were, for the most part, drawn from the poorer classes.

In addition, Jerusalem was undergoing frequent food shortages during this period. Jews from other areas of the Roman world sent donations to Jerusalem for relief of the poor—but Christians could not expect any help from official sources.

Faced with the great need of believers in this first church of the Christian faith, Paul turned to Gentile believers and sought their help. The church in Corinth had been among the first to volunteer to give, but now—much later—they had done nothing to follow through on that earlier pledge.

That is the background of Paul's encouragement to the Corinthians, using the Macedonian church as an example. They provided a vivid illustration of what real Christian giving is all about.

Real Giving Grows Out of Commitment

One of the reasons the Macedonian church offered such an excellent example of faithful giving was that they first gave themselves to God (8:5). You cannot really *give* to God until you have given *yourself to* God.

They "gave themselves first to the Lord." That is the starting point of the Christian life.

Do you remember a few years ago when scandal hit both the Boston and New York Marathons? The winners of the women's races, it turned out, had apparently entered the race near the end. Neither woman had started the race at the beginning and run it to the finish, so both were disqualified. They couldn't win.

In the Christian walk, the starting point is commitment to Christ—yielding your heart and life to God in submission and obedience. Until you give your life to God, any other gift is a mere token, a handout, a tip. God wants *you,* not a weekly check from you.

What is the significance of giving of self in advance of material gifts? Once you have given yourself to God, you understand that what you possess isn't really yours, but God's.

Alan Redpath observes: ". . . They had given themselves up to Him entirely, and when a man comes to a place where he does not own himself, when he comes to that moment in his life when he knows that the grace of the Lord Jesus is such that it did all that for him and therefore he does not own himself, he will never again say that he owns his money. He will never again say that material things belong to him. He belongs to the Lord Jesus himself and therefore everything that he has is Christ's also."[1]

The very word *stewardship* reflects this truth that all we

have is God's. The steward was the housemanager who took care of the master's goods and property on behalf of the master—the true owner.

You and I are stewards. We manage things on behalf of our Master, our Lord, but they all belong to him. And so must we.

In 1939, when the Nazis had reached the pinnacle of power in Germany, a poem appeared in a Berlin newspaper. It represented the militant desire of dictatorship to control the wills of men and women as well as their bodies:

We have captured all the positions
And on the heights we have planted
The banners of our revolution.
You had imagined that was all we wanted.
We want more. We want all!
Your hearts are our goal,
It is your souls we want!

All around us, the battle for our souls still rages. The gods of materialism and power parade before us their claims, crying: "Your hearts are our goal, it is your souls we want!"

Above the conflicting claims we hear another voice—a voice calling us to a higher level, calling us to lay down our lives and receive his, a voice calling us not to exploitation but to redemption, not to power but to service, not to death but to life.

Before any growth can come in the Christian life—before real giving can take place—you and I must commit ourselves to Christ, offering our lives in service and obedience. Then, like those Christians in Macedonia, we will be ready to understand what it means to give.

Real Giving Flows Out of Grace

See how Paul describes giving over and over: in verse 1, ". . . the *grace* that God has given the Macedonian churches"; in verse 6, ". . . to bring also to completion this act of *grace* on your part . . ."; in verse 7: "See that you also excel in this *grace* of giving" (italics added).

In verse 9, Paul offers the ultimate example of grace: Christ emptying himself of all that was rightfully his so that he might reach out to us with God's love.

Grace is love that stoops to save the undeserving. And in verse 1, Paul asserts that the generosity of the Macedonians is proof of the grace they have received from the Holy Spirit. Their giving is simply a reflection of God's redemptive work among them.

Notice three truths about grace:

Grace is a gift of God. As Paul wrote to the church in Ephesus: "For it is by grace you have been saved, through faith—and this not from yourselves, it is the gift of God—not by works, so that no one can boast" (Eph. 2:8, 9).

Just as the grace that drew us to Christ was not of our making but was a divine gift, so is the grace of giving. He extends the challenge, then provides the grace we need in order to respond.

Grace is abundant. There is no limit to grace. As Annie Dillard writes: "You catch grace as a man fills his cup under a waterfall." No matter how much you receive, there is always plenty left.

That's why, as Paul notes, the Macedonian church not only gave according to their means but far beyond their means. They gave beyond what they could afford. That is what happens when the grace of God fills and consumes our lives: we live abundantly, out of the overflow of God's grace and love.

Halford E. Luccock once observed:

Life is justly measured by its overflow. Madame Schumann-Heink was once asked how to sing. She said. "You just fill your lungs with air and let it slop over." There must be more to it than that, for many people have tried that without notable results! But it is true that great music is an overflow. Great living is an overflow. It is the overflow of a filled heart.[2]

When you allow God's grace to take control, you begin to give, to serve, to share out of the overflow.

Grace is directed outward. Grace doesn't attempt to cling to blessings, preserving them for private use. Grace aims outward, sharing with others.

Knowing of the poverty of the Macedonians, Paul had not expected any offering from them. Yet they came to him, begging for the opportunity to be a part of this offering.

If you visit Palestine, you will find two seas, both fed by the Jordan River. Alongside one of them you will find all manner of signs of life: families living, children playing, vegetation growing. By the other sea you will find no sign of life or vegetation—only barren places.

The same river supplies both. Yet for each drop of water that flows into the Sea of Galilee, another flows out. There is a constant movement—taking in and giving out. The result is life.

The other sea jealously guards every drop it receives, not allowing any to flow out. It keeps everything it takes in. We know it as the Dead Sea.

To give is to live. To share is to have life. To hold, to restrict, is to die. Freely we have received; God's grace helps us freely to give.

Real giving grows out of commitment and flows out of grace. There is yet another truth here:

Real Giving Goes Out
Beyond Human Means

The Corinthians to whom Paul wrote were relatively affluent. Not so the Macedonian Christians. Macedonia was one of the most heavily taxed regions of the Roman Empire. In addition the economy suffered the effects of a series of civil wars. In our era, we might compare it to a Third World country, beset with economic difficulties.

On top of this, the Macedonian churches had experienced persecution almost from their birth—and persecution usually included destruction of property and plundering of goods. So these Christians were among the most financially limited of a poor region. Yet out of these tiny resources grew great generosity. Their joy overflowed their difficulties.

Verse 2 is an amazing study of contrasts: "Out of the most severe trial, their overflowing joy and their extreme poverty welled up in rich generosity." Severe trials produced joy! Extreme poverty resulted in generosity!

There is nothing normal or expected here—but then, Christ doesn't call us to normalcy. He calls us to be bold, to be daring, to walk a life of faith.

I like PHILLIPS' translation of verse 2:

Somehow, in the most difficult circumstances, their joy and the fact of being down to the last penny themselves, produced a magnificent concern for other people.

As you have walked with Christ, have you captured that "magnificent concern for other people" which overflows our own limitations and produces a generosity born of grace?

There is a central truth surrounding our stewardship that we should face: God does not *need* our money. It is all his already. He can provide for any need he might wish to meet, but he has chosen to involve us—to empower us with his grace and allow us to be part of this tremendous effort.

1987's "Black Monday" has been compared to the huge 1929 Stock Market crash that contributed to the Great Depression. Prior to the depression, J. C. Stribling was a wealthy Texas rancher. He owned a great deal of land, thousands of head of cattle, and a fortune in stocks and bonds. During this time, he gave $150,000 to build a girls' dormitory on the campus of Mary Hardin-Baylor College, a Baptist school in Texas.

When the depression came, Mr. Stribling lost his entire fortune. He was reduced to virtual poverty.

One day in 1933 a pastor named J. D. Brannon stepped up to the side of an old, run-down Ford, and spoke to

Mr. Stribling and his wife. The pastor explained that he had just returned from taking a carload of girls to the college to begin school. He had spent the night in that dormitory, and wanted to thank Mr. Stribling for his gift to the Christian college.

Mr. Stribling was silent for a few moments as his eyes filled with tears. Then he said, "That was all we saved out of a mighty fortune. It was what we gave away that we were able to keep forever."

Then Stribling added this challenge: "Preacher, tell people to give all they can to the kingdom of God while they have it. I wish I had given more."

God calls us to a commitment of our lives to him. When we are willing to yield our lives to him, then he will give the grace that allows us to give out of the overflow—to give in a way that goes beyond human means. To give to the kingdom of God is investing in the *only* fortune we will be able to keep forever.

14

The Joy of Giving
(2 Corinthians 9:1–8)

Some years ago Alaska experienced an earthquake in which many people were hurt and much property was destroyed. The governor's office received many letters from people demanding official aid for some relative or friend.

The governor's wife remembered one letter that was different. It came from a ten-year-old boy in the Midwest. He had heard about the tragic event and the people in need, so he wrote a letter and enclosed two nickels. In the letter he urged, "If you need more, please let me know."

The apostle Paul had shared with the Gentile churches the story of the great poverty that existed among the Christians in Jerusalem. From the earliest days of the church, there was a commitment to help the poorer members—those who were in great need. The very process of calling out the first deacons was to provide workers to help with this responsibility, allowing the apostles to concentrate their energies on preaching and teaching.

Among the first to volunteer to contribute was the church at Corinth. They were overwhelming in their desire to be a part of this important cause.

Hearing of the Corinthians' commitment to generous support for their Christian brothers and sisters, Paul told other churches—including Macedonia—about this wonderful gesture. Even though their own financial situation was very weak, the Macedonians were inspired by the commitment of the Corinthian church, and they gave also, far beyond their means.

Now Paul is preparing to return to Corinth en route to Jerusalem, and he expects to have some members of the Macedonian church with him. The problem is that following their
early pledge, the believers in Corinth have never followed up
on their good intentions. Thus far there has been no offering.

Have you ever pledged to do something or give something,
then allowed time to pass without action? Most of us can
relate to that: we promise the kids to bring something—and
forget; we assure the boss we will take care of the problem—
then we let the deadline slip by without any action; we promise God we will respond to some need in our lives—then fail
to do so.

So Paul writes this beloved church to encourage their
follow-through on the earlier pledge. How humiliating it will
be, he tells them, to arrive in the company of these Macedonian brothers—to whom he has boasted of the generosity of
the Corinthians (9:1, 2), and who have given themselves far
beyond what could be expected—only to find that no offering
has been gathered! It would be embarrassing for Paul, and
even more embarrassing for the church at Corinth (v. 4).

That is why Paul is sending some of his associates to Corinth—to help them in proceeding with their offering, so that
it will be ready prior to Paul's arrival. It was important for the
Corinthians to have the offering complete before Paul arrived,
lest it look like he was forcing them into something.

Paul wanted the Corinthians to experience for themselves
the joy of giving. In these verses he suggests the manner in
which we may also experience abundant joy in giving.

Give Generously

Paul draws on an agricultural truth to make an important
point in verse 6: "Whoever sows sparingly will also reap sparingly, and whoever sows generously will also reap generously."

Any farmer would recognize the validity of Paul's statement.
It is obvious that, everything else being equal, the size of the
harvest is almost always proportional to the amount of seed

planted. If you only plant four acres of corn, it is highly unlikely you will harvest four hundred acres or even forty acres—you'll harvest no more than you plant.

Imagine a farmer who says to himself: "I'm tired of paying all this money for seed. This year, I'm only going to buy one-tenth my normal amount of seed." So the farmer carries out his plan and only plants 10 percent of his normal crop. In a few months, when harvest time arrives, he goes to his field and cries out in astonishment: "What is this? I've only got ten percent of my normal harvest! Where is all the rest?"

And you and I, looking on at the scene, would say, "Don't be foolish! When you plant less, you'll harvest less. Even city folks can figure that out!"

The principle, as it carries over to giving, is this: when we give to Christ and his church, we are planting seeds that will ultimately produce a harvest. Unless we sow generously, we will not be able to reap a generous harvest of blessing. If we are like the foolish farmer—miserly in our giving—the result will be a miserly harvest of blessing in our lives and in the lives of others we could have blessed.

When we give little, we reap little. That's why Paul urges generosity in giving. What we give is never lost, for it becomes an investment that will produce amazing dividends.

Have you ever seen a chart showing the miracle of compound interest? It's amazing to see how a small amount of money can become a large sum when it is allowed to compound at a reasonable rate of interest. Many people have built significant personal wealth by regularly investing small sums of money and allowing them to grow.

Like a seed sown by a farmer, what we give to Christ is not lost—it is invested. God can use our gifts to produce a great harvest. We never lose by giving generously to God, for it is always returned to us in some way.

Does that mean I "plant" my dollar in the offering plate and God promises to put ten dollars in my pocket? A few years ago a former church member sued his Florida church, saying that the pastor had assured him his tithe would produce a greater return; since he didn't make more money than ever as he had expected, he was suing to get back that tithe!

The truth is, God never tells us to give in order to get back. That kind of giving is not really giving at all—it's simply trading. I give this; God gives that. It's a popular teaching these days; the only problem is, it has nothing to do with the biblical idea of giving.

The harvest we reap may not be material at all. The dividends God gives in your life may have nothing to do with enlarging your bank account or putting a new Cadillac in your driveway.

There are some riches you can bank on, however, when you give generously to God. You can count on the riches of faithfulness and obedience, the riches of love and goodness, the riches of spiritual growth, the riches of God's presence and power in your life. Those are things all the money in the world will never purchase for you. They are a harvest you reap when you sow generously.

There's a legend concerning a wanderer who was on a great journey. As he neared a dry creek bed, he heard God's voice instructing him to gather pebbles there and carry them on his journey. Wanting to be obedient—but not wanting to be weighed down by a load of pebbles—the wanderer picked up a handful of pebbles, placed them in his pocket, and went on his way.

The legend relates that the following morning, many miles away, the wanderer awoke, reached into his pocket, and where he had placed simple pebbles the day before he found precious gems—diamonds, sapphires, rubies. But in the midst of the joy of his discovery, he was sad to realize he could have gathered far more while he had the chance.

Someday we will enter into the presence of God, and the only riches we will possess then are the riches we have sent ahead of us—through generous stewardship, through faithful service. No wonder Paul urges us to give generously if we want to experience the joy of giving.

Give Willingly

Paul wants the Corinthian believers to contribute gener-ously to the offering for the Jerusalem brethren, but he wants it to be an offering that is given willingly, given freely. If it is compelled or forced, the Corinthians will not receive the joy of giving.

When Paul says, in verse 7, "Each man should give what he has decided in his heart to give, not reluctantly or under com-pulsion . . ." that word *reluctantly* literally means "out of pain." Paul doesn't want them to give with a feeling of pain, like taking a bad-tasting medicine. The gift must be given will-ingly or it won't really be a gift at all.

Paul also doesn't want them to give *under compulsion*, as if they feel a burdensome duty to participate in the offering. Have you ever watched a child in church being taught to give? It doesn't always come naturally!

Little Jimmy was in "big church" for the first time, and as the offertory approached his mother began reminding him of the lesson they had discussed at home: that he must put his nickel in the offering plate as a gift to God. The problem is that between home and the choir anthem, his nickel had taken on far more value to Jimmy. He began to be concerned that he was going to have to give God his nickel.

Finally the offertory began, and Jimmy was almost frantic until he saw the usher place the offering plate in front of him. He smiled broadly, stuffed the nickel in his shirt pocket, and passed along the plate. Mother gave him a stern look but held her lecture until after church.

Once the service had ended, she marched Jimmy outside and insisted: "Why didn't you give your offering to God?" Jimmy ingenuously responded: "He never showed up to get it!"

There are Christians who look for any and every excuse to avoid giving back to God what is rightfully his. Joy in giving comes only as we give willingly, without regret or compulsion.

Paul offers a further challenge if we want to experience abundant joy in giving.

Give Cheerfully

The word which our Bible translates "cheerful" is the Greek word *hilaron*. That word, *hilaron*, is the root from which we draw our English word *hilarious*. What an intriguing image that provides: Paul tells the Corinthian believers to "give hilariously." Look up a definition of "hilarious" and you will find it means "noisily merry, boisterous."

Wouldn't you love to see a hilarious offering in church? Just try to imagine, when the pastor says, "Now we come to the time for our offering," the members begin to laugh and smile broadly. People eagerly reach for wallet and purse, and joyfully give their tithes and offerings to God as if it was the most precious privilege on earth. A first-time visitor, used to the more traditional offering, might think he had come to worship with crazy people—or maybe with people who take God's Word seriously.

Why does God love cheerful givers? Because God *is* a cheerful giver! God has cheerfully and lovingly given to us, and he delights in seeing this same spirit active in his children. The ability to be a cheerful giver is an evidence of the grace and presence of God active in our lives.

One minister was urging his congregation to be faithful stewards. He reminded them: "The Lord has done so much for each of us. Each of us should be willing to give him a tenth of our income."

One enthusiastic member—caught up in the spirit of giving—stood and exclaimed, "A tenth just isn't enough! We ought to give a twentieth!"

Although the math may need some work, that's just the spirit Paul challenges us to have. We are to give generously, to give willingly, to give cheerfully. What is the result of that kind of giving?

Paul answers that in verse 8:

God is able to make all grace abound to you, so that in all things at all times, having all that you need, you will abound in every good work.

The message is simple: if we are willing to give, God will make it possible for us to give. He will provide those things we need in order that we might enjoy the blessing and joy of giving. He will bless us that we might have the joy and privilege of blessing others.

In one of his short stories, the Russian writer Dostoevski told of a woman who seemed bound for hell, but would be taken to heaven if she could remember just one unselfish act she had performed during her life.

She thought and thought, but could remember just one act: a time that she had given a piece of withered carrot to a beggar. Soon that same carrot was lowered to her in hell, held by a single string. She frantically grasped the carrot and felt herself beginning to rise toward heaven.

She felt a burden holding her back, and as she looked down, she realized other souls were clinging to her, hoping to go with her to heaven.

"Let go!" she screamed. "This is *my* carrot." And with that, the string broke.

15

War of the Worlds
(2 Corinthians 10:1–6)

Out of an illustrious career, one of the things for which Orson Welles will probably be best remembered is the night he created a war.

It was Halloween night 1938, and many families were gathered around the radio for the "Mercury Theatre" drama. Those who turned on their radios after the program was already underway missed the introduction, explaining that what they would be hearing was a radio drama. All they heard was an amazingly realistic news report that announced aliens from another planet had landed in New Jersey.

To the surprise of Orson Welles and his cast, the next day's newspapers were filled with reports of near hysteria that broke out in town after town. People thought their planet was under attack; they were convinced the "War of the Worlds" was really underway.

Thankfully, no such war took place. Calm was restored, the radio drama ended, and millions of people breathed a collective sigh of relief. There was no war after all.

In chapter 10 of Second Corinthians, Paul is sounding a very different alarm. He wanted the Christian believers in Corinth to understand that they were, in fact, already involved in a "war of the worlds." Though they hadn't yet perceived the danger, the invasion had already begun, and Paul was calling them to prepare for battle. Corinth was to be a battlefield in this cosmic war of the worlds.

Paul often described the Christian life in terms of warfare.

In 1 Timothy 1:18, he provides instruction so that his young brother in the faith can "fight the good fight." In 2 Timothy 2:3, he encourages Timothy, "Endure hardship with us like a good soldier of Jesus Christ." In Ephesians 6:11 and following, Paul talks about putting on "the full armor of God."

Why the military terminology? Paul indicates that we are caught up in a cosmic struggle between good and evil, between the forces of light and the forces of darkness. Each one of us is faced with a decision: Which side of the struggle will we support? Where we will stand in this war of the worlds?

In these verses, Paul suggests a strategy that we must adopt if we are to be true to Christ.

We Trust in God's Power, Not the World's

Every year on May Day, the Soviet Union has a massive parade in the streets of Moscow as a celebration of the nation's military might. Great missiles, powerful tanks, hundreds of well-armed soldiers—all are paraded through the city as a demonstration of Soviet military muscle.

After all, that's the way the world understands power—by showing our muscle. In politics, in warfare, in economics, we learn that you succeed by being stronger and tougher and meaner than the other guy. Nowhere was that more true than the Roman Empire of Paul's day, where the far-flung empire was held together by raw power.

So Paul's manner among the Corinthians had left him vulnerable to attack. The false teachers who had come to Corinth and sought to influence the believers were harshly critical of Paul. "Sure he writes tough letters," they said, "but when he's here with you, he's a wimp!" "He's like a barking dog that runs away when you get near him!" There was nothing subtle about their accusations: they were charging Paul with cowardice.

How do you react when someone accuses you of being a coward? Lots of little boys—and sometimes big boys—get into fights they'd rather not be in, all to prove their "manhood"— to prove they are not cowards.

Paul, on the other hand, had no need to prove his manhood, for he knew that the power on which he depended was not his own. Christ's power and presence were his defense. So Paul begins his statement by reminding the believers of the "meekness and gentleness of Christ." Would they accuse Christ of cowardice because he was gentle and merciful to them? How absurd, then, to question Paul because he had come to them in humility rather than arrogance!

Perhaps Paul was thinking of the words he wrote to the Corinthian church in his first letter to them:

> When I came to you, brothers, I did not come with eloquence or superior wisdom as I proclaimed to you the testimony about God. For I resolved to know nothing while I was with you except Jesus Christ and him crucified. I came to you in weakness and fear, and with much trembling. My message and my preaching were not with wise and persuasive words, but with a demonstration of the Spirit's power, so that your faith might not rest on men's wisdom, but on God's power (1 Cor. 2:1–5).

As Christians our victory is not dependent on our own might or skills, but on the power of God. We can be confident servants and witnesses of the Lord Jesus, because we rest on *his* power.

For many years it was said that a British citizen could travel anywhere in the world in safety, because the power of the British Empire stood behind him. How much more true that is of the child of God!

Like Paul, we can go into a world in need as humble, loving servants. It does not matter what the world around us says or does, for we go forth in the power of the One who holds all of creation in his hands. We emphasize God's power, not our own.

We Walk by God's Standards, Not the World's

In verse 2, Paul reminds the Corinthian church that he is capable of the boldness they think he lacks—but they won't like it when they see it in person. He takes no delight in being severe, but he will be so with those who think he lives according to the world's standards.

I like the way PHILLIPS translates verse 2: "For I am afraid otherwise that I shall have to do some plain speaking to those of you who will persist in reckoning that our activities are on the purely human level."

While he lived *in* the world, with all the difficulties and conflicts that involves, Paul wanted them to see that as Christians we must not live *according* to the world. Christ has called us out from the world's standards and values, to live at a higher level.

That is one of the great challenges we have as Christians: to live *in* the world without being *of* the world. Jesus described it as being salt, giving seasoning to the world; being light, illuminating the darkness of the world; being leaven, making an impact on the world.

Those who make the greatest impact for Christ in our world do not hide themselves away in monasteries or private chambers; they serve Christ *in* the world without becoming *like* the world. Paul lived his faith in the markets and prisons of his world; William Wilberforce carried his faith into Parliament and helped bring an end to slavery in Britain; Mother Teresa lives her faith daily among the poorest of God's creatures.

All around us, men and women who have given their lives to Christ as Lord are serving him faithfully day by day. They are salt and light and leaven in their offices and shops and schools and homes. *In the world* but not living *according to the world.*

Paul says that if we are to be victorious in the war of the worlds, we will trust in God's power, not the world's; we will walk according to God's standards, not the world's.

We Use God's Weapons, Not the World's

When Joseph Stalin was urged to consider the power of the papacy, he asked mockingly, "How many divisions does the pope have?"

That's the way the world looks at power. Mankind has gone from wooden clubs to bows and arrows to neutron bombs, and the search continues for bigger and more powerful weapons that can force others to do our bidding.

God doesn't work that way, Paul says. He points out in verse 4, "The weapons we fight with are not the weapons of the world. . . ."

What kind of weapons does the world use? The world uses force, manipulation, propaganda, political pressure, legislation, military power.

What kind of weapons does God provide? Perhaps the best summary is the one Paul provides in chapter 6 of Ephesians, where he outlines the "full armor of God." There we see the kinds of weapons God's people have been given: truth, righteousness, the gospel, faith, salvation, the Word of God, and prayer (Eph. 6:14– 18).

What a tragedy that all too often the church feels the necessity of abandoning the weapons God has given us in order to adopt the world's agenda. Too many churches have bowed down at the altar of organization, celebrity worship, and the like. Like Esau, we dare to sell our birthright for a moment of exhilaration.

Our generation has seen the churches—on both ends of the political and theological spectrum—move into the political sphere in a dramatic way. First came the civil rights and peace movements on one side, followed by the anti-abortion and school prayer forces on the other. Pity the poor politician who tries to determine what is the real "Christian" position on issues!

The danger, as William Willimon has pointed out, is that "in the church's attempt, right or left, to involve the church in politics to form a better society, we have forgotten the church's more profound political task, which is to *be* a better society. I'm not bothered that Christians are in politics. My problem is that Christians are not in politics on our own terms, from the peculiar standpoint of people who are trying to follow Jesus Christ."[1]

If the church doesn't provide a distinctive model for our society of what it is to live as children of God, all the political activity in the world will be worthless. The church must be a "light to the nations," not simply another political interest group.

What happens when we use the spiritual weapons God has given us?

We demolish the world's strongholds. Anyone familiar with military tactics in Paul's day understood the practice of building strongholds or fortresses. Many Roman philosophers of that day, including Seneca (one of Paul's contemporaries), used the military stronghold as a picture of the mental fortress that could be built in the human mind to protect it from bad fortune.[2]

Paul picks up that same picture and asserts that since these fortresses are in the realm of the will or intellect, only spiritual weapons will be effective in overcoming them. We will never convert someone with a bullet or a ballot—only the Spirit of God can change a heart.

In our day it doesn't take long to see the strongholds that possess men and women and keep them from God. There are intellectual objections—based on some point of philosophy or literary criticism—that people allow to keep them from God. The modern commitment to relativism is a stronghold for many who believe that any religious faith, held sincerely, is perfectly adequate—that there is no "true" or "false" when it comes to matters of the spirit.

The modern spirit of cynicism is a stronghold that leads many to mock the "religious fanatics" or joke about "televangelist scandals"—thus keeping themselves secure from seriously examining the claims of Christ. One of the greatest strongholds of all is the epidemic of noncommitment: people who feel nothing is worth truly giving themselves to, so they wander from cause to cause, from group to group—examining, then moving on without making a commitment.

How can we ever overcome such strongholds? Only through the spiritual weaponry God provides, for it is only as we demonstrate the abundant life in Christ that the world will be drawn to it. Sinful man doesn't seek God, for he wants desperately to be his *own* god. Nothing will break through to him except the Spirit of God working through you and me, demonstrating Christ's love and grace.

When we use God's weapons, we demolish strongholds. More than that:

We take men and women captive for Christ. Literally Paul says we capture the minds of men and women, that they might become obedient to the Lord Jesus Christ.

In every armed conflict, prisoners of war are taken and held. In this spiritual conflict, however, it is the very capture of our minds that actually liberates us. It is only in surrender of my life to Christ that I truly become free.

William Barclay describes an incident that took place among the natives of New Guinea. A certain tribe had a tradition of singing and dancing to "murder songs"; as they reached the climax of the music, they would shout to God the names of the people they wished to kill.

After the members of the tribe were led to Christ, the custom changed. Instead of shouting the names of people they wished to kill, they started shouting to God the names of sins they hated and wanted God to destroy. Literally, a pagan tradition was captured for Christ.[3]

All around us are strongholds to be conquered; all around us are lives that can be captured for Christ. All that remains is our willingness to let God place in our hands his spiritual weapons.

Unlike any other war in history, the outcome of this "war of the worlds" has already been determined. Christ is already victorious. Let's move out as a triumphant army, boldly proclaiming that Good News!

16

Boasting in the Lord
(2 Corinthians 10:7–18)

Did you hear about the golfer who boasted he had just shot a 68 his first time playing at a particular country club? The caddie confirmed the score, and added, "Tomorrow he's going back to play the second hole."

One thing that is common to the human condition is the desire to make ourselves look more important, more significant to other people. So we boast of our accomplishments, we describe circumstances to place ourselves in the best possible light. Whether it's in a locker room or around the office watercooler or even at a Monday-morning ministers' conference, all of us want to be recognized for who we think we are and what we think we've accomplished.

The apostle Paul is dealing with a difficult situation in the Corinthian church. Those who have studied this letter identify chapters 10—13 as a unique section of the epistle. Some even argue that it was written shortly after the first 9 chapters had been sent, following receipt by Paul of further bad news from Corinth.

The problem was an outside group that had arrived in Corinth claiming to be "super-apostles." They boasted of their special status in the church and degraded Paul's status. Their purpose was to assume his role as the spiritual leaders of the Corinthian church.

In the last four chapters of this letter, Paul turns his focus to this group of false apostles who would destroy all that God had been doing in Corinth. His tone becomes quite strong,

and at times Paul becomes sarcastic. The target of his attacks
is not the congregation of believers, but rather this group of
false teachers. Paul's only criticism of the Corinthians themselves is their willingness to listen to falsehoods and suspect
the motives of their first spiritual father.

In these verses Paul launches a powerful counterattack
against the false apostles. He compares the world's boasting
to the call of the Christian to boast in the Lord alone.

The World Seeks Approval
in All the Wrong Places

Several years ago there was a country song that described
"Looking for love in all the wrong places." That's exactly the
indictment Paul places against these false apostles: they are
seeking approval in the wrong places, and trying to seduce
the Corinthian church to follow in their folly.

They seek approval based on surface judgments. The beginning of verse 7 includes a phrase in which Paul challenges
the Corinthians to use some discernment in evaluating the
difference between Paul and these false apostles.

The New International Version translates it: "You are looking only on the surface of things." It is perhaps better translated as an imperative: "Look facts in the face" (NEB); "Look at
what is before your eyes" (RSV); "Do look at things which stare
you in the face!" (PHILLIPS).

It is easy to miss the obvious, isn't it? G. K. Chesterton
tells the story of a criminal who evaded detection though he
was right under the noses of those who were searching for
him—all because he was dressed as a postman. He seemed
too familiar to be noticed.

Caught up in the swirling claims and counterclaims, the
Corinthians were failing to look beyond the superficial. If only
they would look beneath the surface, they would recognize the
genuine quality of Paul's ministry among them, and the false
nature of these intruders.

An example of these superficial attacks is found in verse 10, where Paul notes, "For some say, 'His letters are weighty and forceful, but in person he is unimpressive and his speaking amounts to nothing.' "

His opponents sought to disparage Paul's *moral character.* They interpreted his meekness as weakness, his patience as cowardice. They accused him of being inconsistent—a "tiger" when he's writing letters from a distance, but a "pussycat" when he was present among them.

It is all too true that the world often misinterprets our actions when we truly live for Christ. In a world that glorifies "looking out for number one," the genuine Christian life can be disturbing to people. Gentleness, mercy, compassion can often be misunderstood to be signs of weakness or powerlessness.

When Gandhi began his nonviolent movement to gain India's freedom from British rule, it must have seemed absurd. How could unarmed, nonviolent people free a massive country from a great military power? Yet it was precisely that gentleness which pricked the conscience of the world, including Britain.

Jesus never promises us that the Christian life will be without opposition or difficulty. He does promise that we will be able to draw on a reservoir of power of which the world is totally unaware.

His opponents also sought to disparage Paul's *physical appearance.* Apparently there was much of which they could be critical. Paul was often hampered by ill health, and his body must have shown the marks of beatings and stoning. We know he had a physical defect involving his eyesight, and he had some physical defect identified only as his "thorn in the flesh." A second-century work named *Acts of Paul and Thecla* described Paul as "small, bow-legged, with eyebrows knit together, and an aquiline nose."[1] In case you're wondering, as I did, what "aquiline" means, it is like an eagle's beak: hooked or crooked. No wonder another document from the fourth century calls Paul "bald-headed and hook-nosed."

If someone sent that kind of description to your church in

a recommendation of someone to be pastor, how would you respond? God does not need handsome, blow-dried preachers to do his work. What a shame that we often look only at the surface—the physical appearance—and miss the blessing we could receive from some of God's choicest servants.

Further, Paul's opponents were critical of his *eloquence.* The Greek world put great stress on rhetoric; students spent many hours learning to deliver polished public addresses. Even some of the early Christian preachers, like Apollos, were noted for their oratorical skill.

Then there was Paul, who readily admitted he was no polished public speaker. Indeed his first visit to the Corinthians was marked by "weakness and fear, and with much trembling" (1 Cor. 2:3). In fact Paul felt that his own lack of eloquence gave further evidence of the supernatural power of the gospel, which touched men's lives without any need for a persuasive speaker.

Certainly there is nothing wrong with eloquence. We all would like to have the ability to communicate clearly and persuasively. But the content of our message is far more important than the quality of its delivery. God did not call us to persuade men and women to accept Christ; we are called to be faithful witnesses of the gospel, so that the Holy Spirit might convict and draw people unto Christ.

The world seeks approval based on surface judgments. Paul called on the Corinthians to look deeper.

They seek approval based on their own judgments. Paul strikes a sarcastic note in verse 12 when he says: "We do not dare to classify or compare ourselves with some who commend themselves. When they measure themselves by themselves and compare themselves with themselves, they are not wise."

Paul admits that he is not as bold as these false teachers in at least one respect: he won't use himself as the criteria for congratulation! No wonder the false teachers measured up so well: they used themselves as the measure!

I can run a two-minute mile—if you let *me* decide how long

a mile will be. I can jump twenty feet in the air—if you let *me* determine how long a foot will be.

Can you imagine going into the butcher shop, ordering ten pounds of steak, and having him hand you a tiny portion? You'd say, "This isn't ten pounds!" and he would answer, "It is the way *I* measure pounds!"

How we measure up depends on what the measure is. We need accurate measurements if we want to know where we really stand. Paul says it is no wonder these false teachers commend themselves—they are comparing themselves to themselves!

They are like the young lady applying for a job. The personnel director said, "These are some very good references you have here." The applicant responded, "Why, thank you! I wrote them myself!"

There is always a danger that we might fall into this kind of self-commendation. It is easy to begin thinking, "I suppose I'm not so bad. After all, I don't cheat on my income taxes like Fred, or cheat on my wife like Tom, or cheat on my diet like Bill. Come to think of it, I'm really quite a guy!"

The easiest way to feel confident is to compare ourselves to an inadequate measure. Halford C. Luccock told of a little girl whose mother found her crying furiously because a poor family down the street had moved away. "I didn't know you cared so much for those children," the mother said. But the little girl's answer explained the real problem when she blurted out, "Now there is nobody that I am better than."[2]

That's the crux of the issue, isn't it: we want to find someone we're "better than" so that we can feel superior. Like the false apostles of Corinth, we like to commend ourselves, so we have to use measures of our own making.

Paul reminds the Corinthian believers that there is only one measure by which the Christian is to evaluate his or her life: the measure of Christ. Self-congratulation is meaningless; only that commendation we receive from Christ is of real significance.

As we measure our lives against his, a far more accurate

evaluation emerges. When I measure my pettiness against his greatness, my disobedience against his faithfulness, my self-concern against his compassion, I understand all too well that I simply do not measure up on my own.

The world seeks approval based on faulty measures—on surface judgments and on self-congratulation.

They seek approval based on false claims. Not only were these false apostles trying to lead the Corinthian church astray—they were even claiming for themselves accomplishments that had come from the work of others. That is something Paul will not do, as he says in verse 15: "Neither do we go beyond our limits by boasting of work done by others."

Few things are more tragic than someone trying to live off the glory and accomplishments of others. Yet are there not congregations that do much the same thing—growing only by attracting Christians from other churches, never reaching out to lead new believers to Christ? While there is nothing wrong with someone moving and serving in a new congregation, that adds nothing to the body of Christ—it is redistribution, not growth.

Paul will not boast of such things. He will not seek approval in the wrong places. Where, then, does he say we ought to go for approval?

The Christian Seeks Approval from God

Though he opposes the idle boasting of the false teachers, Paul is not simply trying to reclaim credit or status for himself. Rather, he wants us to understand that our only room for boasting is in what Christ has done in and through us. As he points out in verses 17 and 18: "Let him who boasts, boast in the Lord. For it is not the man who commends himself who is approved, but the man whom the Lord commends."

To boast in the Lord is to glory in God's activity in our lives. We express thankfulness for the work he does through us. Any approval worth having doesn't come from within ourselves or even from other people, but from the Lord Jesus Christ. We live and serve for him.

We see his approval in our lives in the places of service where he allows us to minister on His behalf—as we see lives changed, as we see Christ honored, as we experience the joy of ministry in our own lives. No boasting or human recognition can ever substitute for the power and presence of Christ in your life and mine.

An old tradition that seems to have been lost is the writing of eulogies on tombstones. It is fascinating to go through old cemeteries and read the headstones and wonder about the people memorialized there.

One can well imagine the headstones the false prophets of Corinth would have written for themselves—the messages full of adulation and praise. I suspect that if Paul had been allowed to write his own headstone, the message would have consisted of just six words: PAUL, A SERVANT OF JESUS CHRIST.

There is no greater approval we could find, no more powerful way to be remembered, than as a servant, a minister of Jesus Christ. May God help us to seek that approval and no other.

17

Protecting Us from Ourselves
(2 Corinthians 11:1–15)

O ne of the most famous lines ever spoken on the comic pages came from the mouth of Pogo, when he said: "We have met the enemy, and they is us!"

Isn't that the truth more often than not? We often do more damage to ourselves than anyone else would dream of doing. If you question that, just step on the scales tomorrow morning, then ask why you do that to yourself! I suspect the combined diet most of us eat in sugar, sodium, cholesterol, and all those other goodies does far more harm than all the air and water pollution we will ever encounter.

That same principle applies to the life of the spirit. Paul was concerned about the church at Corinth, a congregation that he founded during his eighteen-month missionary sojourn in the city. The Corinthians were much beloved by Paul, and he continued to correspond with them, trying to provide spiritual direction.

The crisis to which Paul is responding in these verses is the arrival of a group of self-proclaimed apostles who were attempting to lead the church in a different direction than that which Paul had initiated. As we will see in this passage, these false apostles threaten to alter totally the nature and mission of this strategic church.

And worst of all, the Corinthian believers were apparently responding sympathetically to these new leaders. That is why Paul sounds the alarm in these verses, encouraging the Corinthians to be on their guard against this new and dangerous influence. Likewise, we must be alert to dangers which would challenge our effectiveness as servants of the Lord Jesus Christ.

We Must Guard Against Disrupted Faithfulness

As chapter 11 begins, Paul offers a bit of a disclaimer, asking the Corinthians to "put up with a little of my foolishness. . . ." In the preceding verses he has denied the need for boasting, except in the Lord. Now, because of the circumstances in the church at Corinth, Paul feels he must defend his own ministry to them in order to protect them from this new threat to their Christian life and walk. Because the false prophets have extolled themselves and belittled Paul, he feels obligated to do what may be interpreted as "boasting," though he clearly finds it uncomfortable.

Paul is jealous for them, but not for himself; rather, he is jealous that they maintain their devotion to Christ. This is not a jealousy based on ego or concern for one's own reputation; it is a jealousy that arises out of a heart-felt concern for the good of another person.

The image Paul creates in verses 2 and 3 is drawn from the Jewish marriage practices of that day. Marriage actually involved two different events: the betrothal and the wedding ceremony itself. The betrothal was an official engagement that preceded the actual wedding, usually by about a year. Though the man and woman did not yet live together as husband and wife, the betrothal was considered legally binding, and could only be broken by a formal bill of divorcement. Any unfaithfulness by a betrothed girl was considered adultery.[1]

Paul wants the Corinthian church to understand that it is the bride of Christ, and as such was bound to faithfulness to him. Since he had been the one whom God had used to lead most of them to Christ, Paul saw himself as their spiritual father; he wanted to be able to present this bride in all its purity and faithfulness to the bridegroom, Christ, at his return.

Now he fears that these false prophets will seduce the believers away from their previous commitment to Christ. He uses the example of Eve, who was deceived by the serpent in the Garden of Eden and led into sin.

To fully understand the analogy, it is helpful to remember exactly what happened to Eve in that experience. Her seduction was not sexual but mental. First the serpent created questions in her mind about the validity of God's commands. "Did God really say, 'You must not eat from any tree in the garden'?" (Gen. 3:1). Eve knew what God had said, but the serpent's first tactic was to create questions—suspicions—as to God's actual commands.

That happens in our lives, doesn't it? Satan doesn't start by telling us, "God is a liar." He starts by suggesting that we may have misunderstood what God really meant—perhaps God isn't all that concerned as we might think about certain matters. The questioning begins.

Then the serpent said to Eve, "You will not surely die. For God knows that when you eat of it your eyes will be opened, and you will be like God, knowing good and evil" (3:4, 5).

Now the serpent begins a frontal assault on God's commands by encouraging Eve to question God's motives. "Of course God doesn't want you to eat *that* fruit, Eve! *That* fruit will allow you to be just *like* God. Eat that fruit and you'll know everything God knows!"

Satan uses the same strategy in our minds. Facing temptation, our minds suddenly fill with rationalizations—why we really should go ahead with it. After all, it's probably not all that bad. What could happen? Unfortunately, Eve—and soon Adam—learned all too well what happens when we question and disobey God's will for us.

Paul knew that there was a battle underway for the minds of the believers. If the forces of evil could capture their minds—alter the way they thought about the gospel and the things of God—their actions would soon follow. Our minds direct our wills.

What change were these false prophets trying to produce

in the minds of the Corinthian believers? They were offering a different Jesus, a different spirit, and a different gospel than the one Paul originally brought to them (11:4).

The false prophets were probably Judaizers—Jewish Christians who believed that Gentiles had to come to Christ *through* the Mosaic law and Jewish religious system, not apart from them. Some of the Judaizers were more strict than others; it may be that these preachers were not as insistent on the Gentiles' adhering to every element of the Mosaic system. Nevertheless they would have insisted that some actions were required for salvation in addition to accepting God's grace.

That's why Paul warned the Corinthians of the danger of giving their allegiance to a "different Jesus" than the One to whom they have given their lives. As Donald Carson explains:

> As soon as Jesus Christ is not the sole basis for our salvation, as soon as our acceptability before God depends on something more than his sacrifice on the cross, we have denied the sufficiency of his person and work. At that point the Jesus being preached is no longer the biblical Jesus, but an unreal product of human imagination, a relatively powerless figure who cannot effectively save his people from their sins unless they supplement his work with something of their own merit.[2]

That danger is no less real today. Though few of our churches will encounter any "Judaizers," we will most certainly encounter those who preach a "different Jesus" from the Jesus of Scripture.

Some will preach a *sentimental Jesus*—a sweet, gentle figure who makes no demands, who doesn't challenge us, who brings only comfort and warm feelings. Some preach a *legalist Jesus*, who lays out a set of rules and regulations we must follow to satisfy God, with little or no attention to grace. Many in our day preach a *"make-your-own Jesus"*—a vague, shadowy figure to whom we can attach all of our personal attitudes and prejudices, like assembling a plate at a salad bar. This last Jesus makes regular appearances in thousands of pulpits every Sunday!

Yet the only Jesus who can save is the Jesus of the Bible—
the One whom Paul preached to the church at Corinth; the
One who leaps out from the pages of Scripture to claim our
allegiance even today.

As he warned the Corinthian believers, so Paul would alert
us to be on guard against anyone who would preach a different Jesus; who would seduce us into unfaithfulness.

We Must Guard Against Distorted Attitudes

These false prophets sought to establish their own positions by attacking Paul, and in the process revealed terribly
distorted attitudes about the gospel and about our calling as
ministers of the Lord Jesus Christ.

They emphasized human attributes. Paul calls them
"super-apostles" in verse 5, probably reflecting their own
boasting concerning their special status and skills. That is
also reflected in their criticism of Paul, as seen in verse 6:
Paul was not a trained public speaker, as he readily admitted.

The Greeks created schools of rhetoric at which young men
were trained to be polished speakers. These professional rhe-
toricians would ply their trade in the cities of the Graeco-
Roman world, and were well paid for their work. (We have to
remember that this was before television, radio, and the print-
ing press, so speakers *were* entertainment!)

Paul confesses that their accusations about him on this
point are correct; he has never made claims to be a polished
speaker. The word he uses to describe himself was used of a
rhetorical amateur or layman—one who kept to private matters and took no part in public life. But what Paul lacks in
speaking skill he does not lack in wisdom about the things
of God. What the Corinthians know of God's love, what they
understand about the gospel, came from Paul's teaching.

The false apostles emphasize their human skills; Paul em-
phasizes that which God alone can give.

They emphasized personal gain. In the Greek world, the

rhetorician was a professional who received payment for his services. In fact for a speaker to fail to demand payment for his work would create suspicion about his professional standing. The philosopher Socrates was criticized by his contemporaries for refusing to charge for his teaching; to fail to receive financial benefit for teaching was an indication that the teaching itself was worthless.

No one had to worry about these false apostles making *that* mistake! They not only received personal gain for their services—they *demanded* it.

By contrast, during the year-and-a-half Paul lived and worked with the Corinthian believers, he would accept no financial support from them. Rather than be a financial burden on them, he used his skills as a tentmaker to support himself; when that proved inadequate, he accepted gifts from other churches where he had served previously, but he would not allow the Corinthians to pay for his services to them.

Why was Paul so concerned about this, especially since he had taught previously that apostles were deserving of the support of the churches? One factor was the atmosphere in Corinth itself; he didn't want to give any ground to those who might later accuse him of trying to live off the church's largess.

A second factor was Paul's concern for independence. It appears that he never accepted financial support from a church while he was there serving; only after he left that field and began ministry in a new place would he allow the former church to help support his work. No individual or group could ever make claims on Paul based on his financial dependence on them.

Now Paul is being criticized by the false apostles precisely *because* he refused such support. Because Paul's attitude might reflect badly on their own desire for personal profit, they try to cast aspersions on Paul's motives. They even claimed that Paul's independence was evidence that he didn't care about the church! They want Paul to be forced into adopting their method, thereby placing himself at their level.

In the face of such absurd allegations, Paul asks ironically:

"Was it a sin for me to lower myself in order to elevate you by preaching the gospel of God to you free of charge?" Paul lived in poverty in order that the believers might become rich in Christ. In that, he followed the model of Christ, who gave of self rather than gathering things to himself. The life and ministry of Christ is the model for each of us if we are to be effective ministers of his love and grace.

In recent years, the church has been forced to bear the burden of a few well-publicized individuals who have allowed desire for personal gain to overshadow personal sacrifice. The only way for the world to understand that such examples do not reflect the gospel is for us to model the Christ life—for us to place service for Christ above any desire for personal gain or ambition.

The false prophets had distorted attitudes because their focus was on themselves. Paul challenged the Corinthians to be on guard against such falsehood by keeping the focus on Jesus.

We Must Guard Against Deceptive Leadership

A recent survey asked high school students to select individuals they respected the most as today's heroes. At the top of the list were two movie stars: Clint Eastwood and Eddie Murphy—not political leaders or social reformers or ministers, but entertainers! Either our young people have limited exposure to respected leaders, or they have a terrible misunderstanding of what leadership is all about.

The Corinthian church apparently found itself in the same situation, for they were on the verge of following the wrong leaders. Paul uses some of his strongest language to describe these would-be leaders: "For such men are false apostles, deceitful workmen, masquerading as apostles of Christ" (11:13). Where does their deceitfulness come from? Paul says they are simply following their true master: "Satan himself masquerades as an angel of light. It is not surprising, then, if his servants masquerade as servants of righteousness . . ." (vv. 14, 15).

These false prophets will use deceit, manipulation, and treachery, to gain control over the believers in Corinth. Paul urges the church to recognize these "pseudo-apostles" for what they truly are.

In every age, the church must be on guard against those who would deceive and misdirect it. Today there is no shortage of would-be prophets and ministers who make claims for themselves and attract gullible but enthusiastic disciples. There are those who whould shift the church toward new and different callings—to make it an institution of political pressure, or merely a center of moral and religious instruction.

The only protection the church has against such false teachers is to judge all things according to God's will as revealed in his Word. Careful, faithful study of God's Word is the defense we have against those who would deceive and manipulate for their own purposes.

Oswald Sanders, in his classic book on Christian leadership, observed: "True greatness, true leadership, is achieved not by reducing men to one's service but in giving oneself in selfless service to them."

Paul's true greatness as an apostle and as a leader was seen in his absolute commitment to the Lordship of Christ and his sacrificial love for the people to whom he ministered. If we seek to be effective ministers, effective servants of our Lord, Christ calls us to give ourselves for him. That alone is the pathway to authentic Christian service. That alone will produce genuine joy in ministry.

18

The Sufficiency of Grace
(2 Corinthians 12:7–10)

Something often cited as one of the "distinctively American virtues" is self-sufficiency. Our national tradition glorifies the pioneer spirit that led people to strike out into unknown territories and carve a nation out of the wilderness.

We add men like Daniel Boone and Lewis and Clark to our roster of America heroes. Our poets praise the self-sufficient spirit: "I am the master of my fate, I am the captain of my soul." Self-sufficiency is virtually a sacrament in our national religion.

All of this makes it particularly difficult for us to deal with the notion that we may not be so sufficient unto ourselves after all. Yet the gospel itself is based on the reality that we are *not* self-sufficient—that we need something beyond ourselves.

Paul has been forced to confront the false apostles who have invaded the Corinthian church, preaching a corrupted gospel and trying to lead the believers away from the faith in which they were first established. Because the Corinthians were being swayed by the boasting of these charlatans—who claimed amazing spiritual experiences and accomplishments—Paul felt compelled to share some of his own experiences in serving Christ.

All that the false teachers could claim in the way of status and authority, Paul could match and even exceed. In the opening verses of chapter 12, he proceeds to tell of an incredible spiritual experience in which God caught him up to Paradise and allowed him to hear "inexpressible things, things that a man is not permitted to tell" (12:4).

Yet along with that singular spiritual experience came a limitation. Paul goes on to explain, "To keep me from becoming conceited because of these surpassing great revelations, there was given me a thorn in my flesh, a messenger of Satan, to torment me" (v. 7).

The word translated "thorn" is the Greek *skolops*, which referred to something pointed. It could be a thorn, or a stake, or even the pointed end of a fish hook. In the Old Testament, it represented anything that frustrated or created problems for a person. [1]

Over the centuries there have been countless suggestions about what that "thorn in the flesh" might have been in Paul's life. Although some have guessed it may have been some external opposition or internal struggle, most likely it was some type of physical disability. Based on comments Paul makes in this text and elsewhere, suggestions have been made that it may have been bad eyesight, headaches, malaria, epilepsy, or any number of other maladies.

We simply don't have enough information to know for sure the exact nature of Paul's "thorn in the flesh." Whatever it was, it was a source of weakness and frustration for him in his life and ministry. That seems clear from the fact he prayed three times that it might be removed from him.

What was God's response to that prayer? He assured Paul that rather than remove the weakness, the Father could use Paul more effectively *because of* the weakness in his life. Paul learned that man's weakness and God's grace go hand in hand.

How does God use limitations in our lives?

They Keep Us in Touch with Reality

It is all too easy for us as Christians to grow distant from the world in which we live. We can focus our lives around church activities and church friends and lose contact with the world of suffering, hurting humanity that surrounds us.

Paul's visions and spiritual experiences could have had a devastating impact on his ministry, if they had caused him to gain too high a view of himself and become isolated from people as some kind of "super-saint." Instead, Paul's weakness reminded him of his link with humanity, and gave him insights into the needs of people.

In his *A Spiritual Autobiography*, William Barclay tells of the painful death of his mother in 1932. She was suffering from cancer of the spine, and Barclay was struggling with the theological problem of why a good person like his mother had to suffer in such a terrible way.

Her death came during the time he was being licensed as a minister of the gospel. His father said to him, through his tears, "You'll have a new note in your preaching now." Barclay, reflecting on those words many years later, said, "And so I had—not the note of one who knew the answers and had solved the problems, but the note of one who now knew what the problems were."

Paul's "thorn in the flesh" kept him in touch with reality— with the needs and hurts of people whom God loved.

They Keep Us in Touch with Humility

Paul shared with the Corinthian believers the wondrous revelations God gave to him. It was something to which he would cling all his life. The danger was that such an experience could hamper his witness for Christ by giving Paul an exalted sense of his own life and work.

Who among us has not faced the temptation to hold an inflated sense of his own importance? At work, at church, at home, we can fall victim to pride—to consider ourselves a "step ahead" of others.

Paul says God allowed this thorn in the flesh to hamper him to keep him from "becoming conceited" in the face of these incredible revelations. There was apparently something about Paul's nature that would have made him feel exalted and distinctive because of what he had seen and experienced.

God knew that Paul needed something that would remind him of his own limitations.

A potter in his shop may create wonderful, beautiful works of pottery. As each one comes off the potter's wheel, the craftsman examines it for quality. He may have a piece that is particularly well formed and attractive, but he notices a small flaw that will keep it from sitting evenly. In that case, the potter puts it back on the wheel and reshapes it until the flaw is removed.

When we give our lives to Christ, we invite him, as the Divine Potter, to shape our lives to be more like his. God uses limitations and weaknesses that exist in our lives to keep us in touch with reality and to help us retain humility. Further:

They Keep Us Dependent on God

Whatever this thorn in the flesh was, Paul clearly felt it was an obstacle to his full effectiveness. Three times he prayed for God to remove it—paralleling the three times Jesus prayed, while in the Garden of Gethsemane, that *his* impending burden might be removed.

In response to Paul's prayer, we see a tremendous promise contained in verse 9, one of the high points in all of Paul's epistles. There, God assures the apostle: "My grace is sufficient for you, for my power is made perfect in weakness. . . ."

The word for *sufficient* expresses continual availability. God tells Paul—and us—there will never be a shortage of his grace. It will always be adequate to cover every need.

One of the real concerns expressed by farmers and ranchers in the western USA is the growing shortage of water. It may well be that within a few years areas of our nation that have been suitable for farming in the past will become barren and lifeless because the water is gone. Water can run out.

Yet God's grace can never run out. It is like a flowing spring with a limitless source of replenishment. Indeed grace *is* a river that runs from the throne of God and never runs dry. Whatever your need, God's grace is sufficient.

Not only does God promise Paul sufficient grace to meet
his every need, the Lord also provides the apostle with an
insight that will become critical to the effectiveness of his
ministry. God says, ". . . my power is made perfect in weakness" (v. 9).

The word translated "made perfect" or "is perfected" is *tel-
eios*. That's based on the same root word Jesus uses when he
urged us to "be perfect, therefore, as your heavenly Father is
perfect" (Matt. 5:48). The word means the end or limit of
something, finish or completeness.

So God is identifying for Paul the ultimate source of divine
power in our lives: paradoxically, we know God's power at its
greatest strength through our own weakness. Does that mean
God wants us to be weak and timid? No, it means that when
we sense our own weakness, at that point we open our hearts
to allow God's power to work. God cannot use people who are
convinced of their own self-sufficiency; God's power is most
clearly seen in the lives of those who recognize their own weakness and, therefore, seek God's presence and power in their
lives.

So Paul glories in his own weakness, not because of any
perverse pleasure in his own pain or affliction, but because
those very weaknesses had opened the door more fully for God
to enter and work. Have you ever tried to pour more water
into a glass that was already full? Nothing more can be added
to a glass that's already full. And God cannot enter and work
with power in a life that's already filled with self.

Paul willingly endured the thorn in the flesh and other difficulties, because God's power was magnified at the very point
of his weakness, ". . . For when I am weak, then I am strong"
(12:10). The false apostles boasted of their accomplishments
as signs of their own power and authority; Paul boasts instead
of his weakness, because through that weakness God made
himself known.

Have you ever prayed asking God to remove some problem
or difficulty from your life, and it is still there? Perhaps it is
a physical affliction, a limitation in some area, a challenging

environment. Could it be that God has not removed that thorn from your life because he desires to use it to demonstrate his power *through* your weakness?

A new farmer employed a professional well-digger to create a well on his property. The agreement was that the landowner would pay for the digging by the foot—the deeper the well had to go before finding water, the more it would cost.

Fortunately, the digger struck a modest supply of decent water after only about ninety feet. He assured the farmer that the water supply should normally be sufficient. Delighted at the thought he had saved money with such a shallow well, the farmer paused over that word *normally*. While that might be acceptable nine years out of ten, what would happen in a particularly dry season. Would it be sufficient then?

"No, sir," the well-digger answered. "To be sure of that, we'll have to go down until we strike the deep streams, those big reservoirs far underground." Then the digger reminded the farmer, "But that will cost you more."

Digging deeper always costs more. Faith can stay at a surface level—full of sweet God-talk and lots of "warm fuzzies"—but when the days of crisis come, that kind of faith blows away with the dust. Surviving the hard times requires a durable faith, able to withstand the storms and thorns that inevitably come our way. For that we must dig deeper.

God allows the limitations and weaknesses of life to touch us to help us dig deeper, to become stronger, to become greater servants of the Lord Jesus. Because it is in our weakness that God's power is seen most clearly.

19

Renew the Joy
(2 Corinthians 12:11—13:5)

The movie "Rocky" (and its sequels) have been so successful because they touch a part of us that loves to see a person overcome adversity and emerge victorious.

What is more exciting than seeing a basketball team come back, after being down twenty points at the half, and win the game at the final buzzer? Or seeing a baseball team in the World Series, after being down four or five runs, to rally in the ninth inning and win the game?

The sports world is full of such stories—individual competitors or teams making a dramatic comeback, mobilizing all their energies and skills to achieve victory in the face of certain defeat. There's something heartwarming about a comeback story, isn't there?

Paul is greatly concerned about the danger in which the Corinthians have placed themselves and their faith. Their acceptance of the "false apostles" into their church—preaching a message that corrupted the authentic gospel Paul had brought them—was heartbreaking to Paul. He loved these brothers and sisters in Christ, and wanted them restored to a right relationship with Christ and with himself.

Paul is providing a final, urgent plea for the believers to renew their joy in Christ by setting things right in their lives and in their church. The principles provided to the Corinthian church are just as valid today as then. If you feel the need to renew the joy in your own life, these actions will bring

138

a new power, a new strength, a new joy to your Christian life and ministry.

Recognize Authentic Leadership

One of the major threats to the Corinthian church was the ready acceptance of a group of "false apostles" into their midst. These new preachers taught a distorted gospel, and sought to secure financial gain from the churches. To enhance their own status, they ridiculed Paul and attacked his life and teaching.

Of all the early churches no congregation should have been quicker to rise to Paul's defense than Corinth. He had spent eighteen months living and working among them, supporting himself by manual labor to avoid being a burden to them. He had loved them, prayed with them, led them to faith in Christ. And now, as a group of exploitive and deceitful teachers attack Paul, his beloved church stands silently by and listens. How it must have broken Paul's heart to learn that these brothers and sisters for whom he had given so much of himself had failed to defend him in the face of such attacks.

All they had to do was make a simple comparison of the false apostles with Paul to realize that Paul was in no way inferior to these intruders (12:11). Their very Christian lives were the greatest evidence of the validity of Paul's apostleship; *they* were Christians because of his witness.

It is so easy to get swept up in a ground swell of support for a popular new teacher or preacher or movement. There are professing Christians who go from church to church, from revival to revival, looking for a new "spiritual high" to keep them going. The problem is, those "highs" eventually become less and less satisfying. Like a heroin addict, each successive "fix" requires more and more of the drug to satisfy.

Paul reminds the Corinthians that they had seen the "signs, wonders and miracles" of apostleship in his own ministry also, but with one great exception to the work of the false apostles—Paul's signs were done "with great perseverance"

(12:12). Unlike the pseudo-apostles, Paul's ministry among
them was marked by patience, endurance, a willingness to
suffer affliction on their behalf. All that was forgotten by the
Corinthians; as Donald Carson observes, "they wanted miracles without suffering, triumphs without endurance."[1]

The church today also needs to show extreme care in recognizing authentic spiritual leaders. There are many who
would grasp leadership, only to corrupt the faith and the
church as the false apostles did in Corinth. How are we to
recognize authentic spiritual leaders? Drawing on Paul's life
and teaching, we might consider several tests:

1. *A Christ-like life.* Authentic spiritual leaders don't spend
time boasting of their own piety or great spiritual experiences;
their lives demonstrate those characteristics. A leader who
spends much time discussing his or her own credentials—
rather than Jesus Christ—is more akin to the false apostles
than to the genuine variety.

2. *Faithfulness to the Word.* The written revelation of God
in Scripture is a safeguard against those who would distort
the gospel for their own ends. It is vital for Christians to spend
the necessary time in the Word which will allow them to recognize abuse or misinterpretation of the text.

Most quasi-Christian cultic groups make a great use of
Scripture—but only as isolated verses, torn out of their nat-
ural context and strung together to create altogether new
meanings. Many university-based cults target young people
from evangelical churches—they have grown up accepting the
authority of Scripture, but few know that same Scripture well
enough to recognize its misuse.

3. *Focus on Christ.* The false apostles boasted of all the
signs and wonders "they" performed. In contrast, Paul does
not claim any signs of his own; rather, he says they "were
done among you" (12:12) by God. False leaders focus on themselves, their own work, their own organizations; authentic
Christian leaders focus on Christ.

4. *Commitment to those served.* As a minister of Christ,
Paul gave himself in service to people. Unlike the false apostles,

he never became a burden on the Corinthian church (v. 13); rather than taking from them, he gave.

Paul would have been well within his rights to accept financial support, but he refused to ask for or accept such aid, in order that he might not harm his witness among the suspicious Corinthians. He was committed to reaching them for Christ, even at the cost of his own needs.

One of the keys to renewing the joy of service for Christ is recognizing and following authentic spiritual leaders.

Rediscover Focus

In verse 14, Paul reminds the Corinthians of an important truth in the Christian life: God doesn't want our things; he wants *us*.

Paul is coming back to Corinth, not to take their financial resources, but to help them rediscover their focus on the Lord Jesus Christ. The Judaizers or false prophets had likely been emphasizing human activity: ceremony, law, regulations. Paul seeks to redirect their vision to Christ alone, the only hope of salvation.

We, too, may be guilty of distorting our focus. We may even spend the majority of our time concentrating on the *good* while we miss the best: Jesus.

We can focus on *activities*. We serve on the church board, sing in the choir, teach Sunday school, work in the nursery. There are a thousand-and-one activities in every local congregation, and each job is important. Yet there is always a danger of placing our primary focus on the job at hand and lose contact with the One whom we serve.

We can focus on *money*. Material possessions have great meaning to us. We may claim to have little concern for "things," but few of us will volunteer to give up air conditioning in July, trade our automobile for a horse, or try the latest fashions in wild animal skins and fig leaves.

The greatest danger lies in the growing preoccupation with money that can cause us to focus on self and not God. Little by little we can allow materialism to assume center stage, and push Christ to the side.

We can even focus excessively on *worship*. God calls us to worship him, and some of our highest spiritual moments come during times of corporate worship. The magnificent songs of praise, the inspiring prayers, the powerful proclamation of God's Word—all of these can lead us into the very presence of God.

Yet it is possible—especially for pastors and other worship leaders—to become so caught up in the *mechanics* of worship that we lose touch with the *meaning* of worship in our own lives. In the act of drawing a congregation into a spirit of worship, it is possible for leaders to lose touch with worship in their *own* lives.

There are many good things to claim our attention, but we must be careful to keep our primary focus on Jesus if we are to renew the joy in our lives and ministry.

Restore Relationships

Notice the father-child relationship Paul assumes in these verses: ". . . After all, children should not have to save up for their parents, but parents for their children. So I will very gladly spend everything I have and expend myself as well . . ." (12:14, 15).

Paul has enjoyed a wonderful relationship with the Corinthian Christians. He had been a spiritual father to them; they had been his spiritual progeny. Yet, as a result of the false apostles' work, the Corinthians had begun to question Paul's motives. They had allowed barriers to emerge in their relationship with Paul.

In these verses, we observe some keys to restoring relationships. The first is *love*. Paul's love for them is so great that he is willing to give of himself with no expectation of anything in return. Like a father, he will provide for his children, not expecting them to provide for him (as the false apostles did).

We all need to know we are loved—to know that someone

cares. One father came up with a creative idea: instead of reading the same bed-time stories to his little daughter each night, he recorded her favorite stories on tape.

Presenting the tape recorder to her, he said, "Now you can play your stories whenever you want. Isn't this wonderful?"

The little girl replied sadly, "No. It hasn't got a lap!"

We all need a lap. We all need to be loved. Paul seeks to restore his relationship with the Corinthians by reminding them of his love for them.

Another key to restoring relationships is *trust*. The false apostles had accused Paul of deceitful motives, and now the people themselves had begun to question their spiritual father, although they should have known better.

Lack of trust produces strain in a relationship, and can often result in relationships being completely broken. The American political landscape since Watergate has shown the devastation that results from lost trust. Once they lost confidence in the integrity of our national leaders, many Americans lost confidence in the political process itself, and each year fewer eligible voters show the concern even to vote.

Apparently the false apostles suggested that Paul was going to skim a profit for himself from the offering they were taking for the Jerusalem believers. That is the likely basis for Paul's statement "Crafty fellow that I am, I caught you by trickery!" (v. 16). He was probably simply echoing the accusations being made against him, though with no evidence of any misconduct.

Paul reminds the believers in Corinth they had no reason to mistrust him. He had spent eighteen months among them— had he given them any reason to doubt his integrity? He sent Titus and others to work among them on his behalf—had these men done anything worthy of mistrust (12:17, 18)? The answer was clearly *no*—by first-hand experience, the Corinthians knew they could trust Paul and his ministry among them.

A third key to restoring relationships is *selflessness*. The strongest relationships are built on a spirit of giving and not

taking. Paul says, "So I will very gladly spend for you everything I have and expend myself as well . . ." (v. 15).

The word Paul uses for *spend* meant to use completely, to
exhaust. Literally he was expressing his willingness to sacrifice himself—even his own life—on their behalf. The Corinthians had only to compare Paul's selfless attitude to the
grasping attitude of the false apostles in order to realize the
difference between them.

Selflessness builds relationships. As we willingly give of
ourselves for another, a bond of love and commitment is built.

A man came out of a store to his new car, only to find a
young boy looking at the automobile. "Mister, how much did
you have to pay for this car?" the boy asked.

"I didn't have to pay anything," answered the man. "My
brother gave me this car as a gift."

The boy pondered that information for a moment, and then
responded, "Boy, I wish I could be a brother like that."

If we want to restore relationships, we must be brothers
like that—willing to abundantly give of ourselves to others.

Love, trust, selflessness—all of these things existed in Paul's
relationship with the Corinthian church. They needed only to
remember these things to restore a sense of joy to that
relationship.

Repent of Sin

Nothing can stifle the joy of the Christian life more than a
spirit of carnality—allowing sin to again gain a stronghold in
a life that has been committed to Christ. Paul's first letter to
the Corinthians is filled with warnings about leading carnal,
sinful lives while claiming to follow Christ. Now Paul fears
that the same spirit of carnality—which had been controlled
for a time—may be returning to Corinth.

The sins Paul cites in verse 20: "quarreling, jealousy, out-
bursts of anger, factions, slander, gossip, arrogance and disorder"—and   in   verse 21—"impurity,   sexual   sin   and

debauchery"—are the same sins that occupied so much of Paul's attention in that first epistle.

The only answer is *repentance.* The believers in Corinth must repent of such sin—seeking God's forgiveness and turning away from these actions.

The Christian life that is marred by sin is not a life of joy; rather, it is filled with guilt, anxiety, regret. Why? Because when you surrender your life to the Lordship of Christ, the Holy Spirit comes to abide in your life. The Spirit provides guidance and direction, and the Spirit also provides the strength to remain true to our high calling as Christ's followers. When we fall short of God's will, the Spirit works in us to draw us back to the Father. The Holy Spirit will not refuse to let you sin—but if you do allow sin to dominate your life, the Holy Spirit will continually pull at your conscience, calling you back to your high calling in Christ Jesus.

The Corinthians were allowing sin to regain a foothold in their lives—but there was no joy among them. Paul called them to repent of sin, in order that God might renew the joy of their salvation.

There was one other appeal which Paul laid before his beloved Corinthian church.

Return to Christ

One of the primary themes of Paul's second letter to the Corinthians is the paradox of power and weakness. The false apostles came to Corinth claiming to possess power, but events would ultimately reveal their true weakness—they did not speak for Christ but for themselves.

Paul, on the other hand, came to the Corinthians acknowledging his own weakness. Yet in his weakness, Paul would ultimately be shown to have the greatest strength, because God's power would be made complete in Paul's weakness.

In this Paul is following the model of his Lord. As he says in verse 4 of chapter 13: "For to be sure, he was crucified in weakness, yet he lives by God's power. Likewise, we are weak in him, yet by God's power we will live with him to serve you."

Now it is time for the Corinthians to decide for themselves. Will they respond to an appeal to human power or to a different appeal: a call to human weakness that results in divine power? They can place their allegiance with the false apostles—or they can return to Christ. Though the critics had questioned Paul, it is the believers in Corinth who must examine their own lives, to see if they are "in the faith" (13:5).

The Christian life, if it is to be joyful and victorious, requires constant self-examination to be sure we are being true to Christ. William Graham Sumner was an Episcopal minister who joined the faculty at Yale University. Years later he wrote that when he began his study in sociology, he put his religious faith away in a drawer; when he went back to look for it a few years later, it was gone. It had evaporated![2]

It is a tragic reality that we can allow our faith to sit on a shelf, gathering dust, until it no longer plays a dynamic role in our lives. How many men and women are now in midlife or beyond, the enthusiastic faith of their youth now just a distant memory. Though there remains a gnawing anxiety that something in life is missing, still they remain apart from Christ.

Perhaps that describes your life today. Though Christ once played a central role in your life, that is no longer true. Other priorities have pushed him from the pre-eminent place in your heart. Business, personal pleasure, family concerns, ambition—any of these—or maybe something altogether different, has taken center stage in your life.

Today you can return to Christ. The joy you once experienced as a follower of Jesus Christ can be rekindled in your heart. Though they had made terrible mistakes, it was not too late for the Corinthians to rediscover the power and purpose Christ could bring to their lives. It is also not too late for you. Will you allow the Lord to renew the joy in your life this very day?

20

Final Thoughts
(2 Corinthians 13:11–14)

In a symphony there is often a recurring theme—a memorable musical phrase that occurs again and again throughout the work, returning like a familiar friend. Though the composer may produce variations on that theme—couching it in different styles, using different instrumental combinations, and so on—the familiar theme still strikes a responsive note in our ears and our minds.

As composer of this second letter to the church at Corinth, the apostle Paul provided a central theme—joy in ministry—and proceeded to return to that theme again and again. He uses different phrases, explores different facets, but still the theme is there: Christ calls us to experience joy as we minister in his name.

Now as Paul draws his letter to a close in these verses, he returns to that theme for a final time. The word in verse 11, which is normally translated "farewell," has another meaning also. It is frequently used to mean "rejoice." The same word is found in Philippians 3:1: "Finally, my brothers, *rejoice* in the Lord!" The same word is found in 1 Thessalonians 5:16: "Be *joyful* always" (italics added).

I believe Paul is drawing this epistle to a close with a final encouragement to the Corinthian believers to serve Christ joyously. So these final four verses actually begin, "Finally, brothers, rejoice!"

What will produce in the Corinthians the capacity to rejoice? Paul suggests three traits that ought to characterize

147

their lives as individuals and their corporate life as a church—
elements which will produce a sense of joy in our lives as well.

We Are Called to Obedience

The first injunction Paul offers in verse 11 is "Aim for per-
fection." The phrase has been translated "be perfect" (KJV),
"perfect your lives" (KNOX), "mend your ways" (RSV).

It is interesting to note that the same verb is found in Mark
1:19, where we read that James and John were "in a boat,
preparing [or *mending*] their nets." The word suggests repairing or fixing something. It is an active word; there is
something they must *do.*

Already in this letter Paul spelled out actions which must
be taken by the Corinthian believers to again be in the center
of God's will for their lives. They must be faithful in complet-
ing the offering for the poor in Jerusalem; they must rid themselves of any immoral practices; they must reject the corrupted
gospel taught by the false apostles and affirm Paul's authority
among them.

Obedience must move beyond good intentions and result
in specific actions. We must cross the line from plans to
performance.

John Woolman was a Quaker who had no real concern
about slavery until the day when his job required him to prepare a bill-of-sale for a female slave. That event began a process
in his life that would eventually make John Woolman an out-
spoken opponent of slavery. He did more than express concern, however; he acted.

Albert Schweitzer was a brilliant man—a man of great
learning and great faith. Yet he knew that faith was incomplete
until put into action, so he gave his life in service to the people
of Africa.

Apart from obedience to God's will, there is no growth in
grace, no maturing in our Christian walk. Obedience is a gate-
way, which when open, allows God's joy to enter our lives. We

are called to obedience—putting our faith into action day by day.

We Are Called to Unity

When Paul urges the Corinthians to "be of one mind" (13:11), he is not telling them to place their intellect on a shelf and mindlessly follow himself or any other teacher. Jesus told us to love God with our minds; one of the ways we serve Christ is by developing our God-given minds in order to better honor him.

What Paul seeks in his call for "one mind" is a unity of purpose, a singleness of concern. They were to be unified in the mind, implying an agreement on the truth. Though they had different abilities, different personalities, different lifestyles, the believers were to find common ground around the reality of Jesus Christ as Lord.

What an amazing assortment of Christian denominations exist just in the United States! In most any metropolitan area you can browse through the Yellow Pages under "Church" and come across dozens of different denominations and groups, many claiming the name "Christian." Compared to a few generations ago, when many American towns gave you a choice between "Baptist" and "Methodist" (and the Presbyterians had to go to the next town over), we enjoy an incredible diversity within the Body of Christ.

Yet whatever our denominational label, we are called to unity—to "be of one mind" in Christ Jesus. There are some thoughts, some beliefs, that must be commonly held among us for the word "Christian" to have any meaning.

In our day it is common to hear someone say, "It doesn't really matter *what* you believe, as long as you're *sincere.*" Such a sentiment sounds so tolerant, so modern—and is so foolish. Suppose I sincerely believe I can jump from the top of the World Trade Center and float to the ground without injury. Would that sincerity protect me from the law of gravity?

We live in a pluralistic society, and part of our American

heritage is respect for the right of others to believe differently than ourselves. Yet the testimony of Scripture is that *what* you believe *does* make a difference. A person can be *sincere,* and be *sincerely* wrong!

As Christians we have invested our lives in the belief that some beliefs are true, and that in this truth is the hope of life abundant and life eternal. We are committed to the truth of Jesus' life, death, and resurrection. We are committed to the truth of his ultimate power and Lordship in history and in our lives. We are committed to the truth that only through repentance, forgiveness of sins, and submission of our lives to Jesus Christ can we know the power and presence of God in our own lives.

However we may differ on other issues—important though they may be—as those who claim the name of Christ, we must "be of one mind" around these central truths of Scripture. Once we experience this unity, we are able to respond to Paul's final challenge in these verses.

We Are Called to Cooperation

Unity of thought is not enough; that unity must be put into practice. That is why Paul follows the injunction to "be of one mind" with the additional challenge, "live in peace" (v. 11).

The Corinthian church had not known a great deal of peace in its young life. As we observe in both Paul's letters to this congregation, the believers in Corinth had become embroiled in factions, disputes, lawsuits with one another, controversy and disorder even in their worship services. We can only imagine what non-Christians in Corinth must have thought of this young religion when they observed the disunity that existed among its followers!

Paul knew how vital it was that they blend mind, heart, and life in a spirit of cooperation. Christians must show the rest of God's creation that it *is* possible for people to live in peace— through the presence of the Prince of Peace in their hearts. Unless we can work hand in hand on behalf of our common

Lord and Savior, we have little to share with a lost and dying world.

Once we are of the same mind—united in a common allegiance to the Lordship of Christ—we are freed from petty bitterness and conflict. In Christ we are freed to work together, to serve together, to "live in peace."

One of the tragedies farmers fear for their children is becoming lost in a cornfield. The tall stalks of corn, the long rows that all look alike—these dangers can cause a child (or an adult) to become disoriented and wander in circles.

One mother experienced the reality of that terrible fear when her little daughter, just a toddler, wandered from the porch and into the cornfield nearby. As soon as the mother realized what had happened, she began to search but without success. She called some neighbors, and they ran up and down the rows of corn, calling the little girl's name—but with no reply.

After hours of searching without success, one of the neighbors suggested a new strategy. They called in additional helpers, then lined up along the edge of the cornfield and joined hands. Linked together, they began to move systematically through the rows of corn until the little girl was discovered— tired and frightened, but well.

As that relieved mother led her precious daughter back to the house, she said to her neighbors, "If only we had joined hands earlier!"

That is what Paul is trying to communicate to his beloved church in Corinth. If we will join hands in service for Christ, we will accomplish so much more than if we try to go our separate ways.

If you have ever cooked over an outdoor grill, you know that one of the steps in preparation is to bring the charcoal briquettes together for lighting. You don't lay one here, then another there, then a third still farther away—all that would do is produce a series of small, short fires. By bringing the charcoals together, they work in unison to create a great blaze. In fact, the only time you move the charcoals far apart from one another is when you are ready for the fire to go out.

When Christians move apart, the fire goes out. When we work together for God's glory, the Spirit is able to stir our efforts into a mighty blaze.

To know true joy in ministry, we are called to obedience, unity, and cooperation. As these characteristics become part of our daily walk with Christ, Paul says. ". . . the God of love and peace will be with you" (13:11).

We experience God's presence through responding to his call. No wonder Paul implores the Corinthians to "listen to my appeal," for they will never know true joy in ministry apart from obedience to Christ, unity with fellow believers, and cooperation in the work of the kingdom.

There is no more vital message Paul could have left for us today. In a world filled with conflict and disorder, the church must be a source of warmth and light and peace. Sinful men and women must learn what it means to follow Christ by observing the obedience of our lives. Angry, bitter people will only learn the power of unity as they see God's love draw us together as one. Ambitious, frustrated folks can only experience the reconciling power of God's peace as they see cooperation modeled in our lives as Christians.

It is not easy. It is never easy. But the goal—the abundant joy we experience in knowing and serving Christ—makes the journey worth the cost—any cost.

Source Notes

Chapter 1 Marks of a Servant

1. Helmut Thielicke. *How the World Began* (Philadelphia: Fortress Press, 1961), pp. 183, 184.
2. Charles Colson. *Who Speaks for God?* (Winchester, IL: Crossway Books, 1985), p. 15.

Chapter 2 The Divine "Yes"

1. E. Stanley Jones. *The Divine Yes* (Nashville: Abingdon Press, 1975), p. 7.
2. This follows the approach of C. K. Barrett in *The Second Epistle to the Corinthians* (New York: Harper & Row, 1973). Barrett suggests two possibilities relating to this "painful visit": (1) an unannounced visit, which caused Paul to abandon plans for the announced double visit; (2) the first of the two visits "ran into trouble in Corinth" and Paul therefore abandoned the second planned visit. Barrett favors the second interpretation because it "suits the 'not again' . . . of verse 23, and fits well into Paul's justification of himself" (p. 86).
3. Ibid., p. 79.
4. A. T. Robertson. *Word Pictures in the New Testament*, Volume IV (Nashville: Broadman Press, 1931), p. 240.
5. Jones. *The Divine Yes*, pp. 110, 111.

Chapter 3 The Fragrance of Christ

1. William Barclay. *The Daily Study Bible: The Letters to the Corinthians* (Philadelphia: The Westminster Press, 1954), pp. 204, 205.
2. A. T. Robertson. *The Glory of the Ministry* (Nashville: Broadman Press, 1979), p. 42.

3. From "Mission to Modern Macedonia," a sermon by Richard Cunningham, published by Southern Baptist Theological Seminary, Louisville, KY.

Chapter 4   A Letter of Christ

1. Philip E. Hughes. *The Second Epistle to the Corinthians* (Grand Rapids: Wm. B. Eerdmans Publishing Co., 1962), p. 86.
2. Allen Dixon. *Reader's Digest* (November 1977), p. 136.

Chapter 5   When the Veil Is Lifted

1. Barrett. *The Second Epistle to the Corinthians*, p. 122.
2. Alan Redpath. *Blessings Out of Buffetings* (Westwood, NJ: Fleming H. Revell Company, 1965) pp. 46, 47.

Chapter 6   We Have This Treasure

1. *The Commission,* June-July 1985, S. B. C. Foreign Mission Board.
2. Barrett. *The Second Epistle to the Corinthians*, p. 128.
3. Hughes. *The Second Epistle to the Corinthians*, p. 123.

Chapter 7   The Coming Glory

1. George R. Beasley-Murray. "Second Corinthians," *Broadman Bible Commentary,* Volume XI (Nashville: Broadman Press, 1971), p. 36.
2. Colin Kruse. "The Second Epistle to the Corinthians," *Tyndale New Testament Commentaries* (Grand Rapids: Wm. B. Eerdmans Publishing Co., 1987), p. 117.

Chapter 8   Why Share Christ?

1. French L. Arrington. *The Ministry of Reconciliation* (Grand Rapids: Baker Book House, 1980), p. 82.

Chapter 9   The Tragedy of Delay

1. Bruce Thielemann. "Claiming the Molten Moment," *Christianity Today*, February 1, 1985, pp. 30, 31.

Chapter 10   Confidence in Ministry

1. Gerhard Kittel, ed. *Theological Dictionary of the New Testament*, Volume IV (Grand Rapids: Wm. B. Eerdmans Publishing Co., 1967), pp. 581, 582.
2. Barclay. *The Daily Study Bible*, p. 240.

Chapter 11   Joy in Ministry

1. F. F. Bruce. *The New Century Bible Commentary: I & II Corinthians* (Grand Rapids: Wm. B. Eerdmans Publishing Co., 1980), p. 217.

Chapter 12   When Bad News Becomes Good News

1. Robertson. *Word Pictures*, p. 240.

Chapter 13   What Real Giving Means

1. Redpath. *Blessings Out of Buffetings*, p. 149.
2. Halford E. Luccock. *More Preaching Values in the Epistles of Paul* (New York: Harper & Brothers Publishers, 1961), pp. 91, 92.

Chapter 15   War of the Worlds

1. William H. Willimon. "Mixing Religion and Politics," *Preaching*, Volume IV, No. 3 (November-December 1988), pp. 19, 20.
2. Kruse. *Tyndale New Testament Commentaries*, p. 174.
3. Barclay. *Daily Study Bible*, pp. 268, 269.

Chapter 16   Boasting in the Lord

1. Robertson. *Word Pictures*, p. 254.
2. Luccock. *More Preaching Values*, p. 102.

Chapter 17   Protecting Us
from Ourselves

1. Kruse. *Tyndale New Testament Commentary*, p. 183.
2. Donald A. Carson. *From Triumphalism to Maturity* (Grand Rapids: Baker Book House, 1984), p. 88.

Chapter 18   The Sufficiency of Grace

1. Kruse. *Tyndale New Testament*, p. 205.

Chapter 19   Renew the Joy

1. Carson. *From Triumphalism to Maturity*, p. 157.
2. Luccock. *More Preaching Values*, p. 122.